<u>The Truth</u>

It feels strange to say, but human beings have become the only species on the planet which does not live in harmony with nature. You don't need to be some tree-hugging hippy to notice that we've actually taken this inharmonious relationship to a level of destruction. We're long past petty discussions of electric automobiles and plastic straws. We aren't going to save ourselves with less toilet flushes.

We do not inherit the Earth from our ancestors, we borrow it from our children. No need for drastic action; we simply need to be responsible for what we produce because it will ultimately require disposal. We can't eliminate waste from society, but we can put things in the right place.

Sometimes it only takes a few people and a bit of ambition to start a movement. Three seemingly uninteresting characters managed to make the entire world look at their load before dumping in the trash. A frustrated journalist, a minimum-wage cook, and a food bank volunteer crossed paths and managed to light a fire that stinks like a landfill. Their story will come soon.

The dumps are overloaded, and they have been this way for a while. Two of the biggest contributors to this waste are plastic and food, both of which can be easily controlled. Our problems have just been hidden away from us, and the discussions seem to die out before they really begin. Somehow, the human race has managed to interfere with the natural processes of growth and decay, a fundamental element of life itself.

Our uneaten food does not belong in the garbage. Food waste generates the same amount of greenhouse gases as thirty-seven million cars. Most of the disposed food is edible, and if it can't be fed to a human being or an animal, it should be composted or converted to energy. Food is an entirely separate category of waste, but only a few places in the world have managed to recognize it yet.

Plastic is not, never was, and never will be, recyclable. Every single thing we have been told by the government and plastic makers about recycling is gibberish. 90% of all plastic ever produced has not even been *attempted* to be recycled. The rough estimate suggests that amount of plastic is **thirteen trillion pounds.** Easily understandable, a plastic machine can spit out over 300 pounds of plastic in about sixty seconds.

When recycled, a piece of plastic degrades, making it useless. Nearly all types of plastic can only be recycled one time, and that process is expensive. We will never solve our problem with recycling, and the industry is well aware of this fact. The real way to handle this issue is regulation of the industry; previous laws were allowed to expire over the past thirty years. We are now seeing the results.

Left in the environment, plastic does not biodegrade like organic products. Instead, it photodegrades from sunlight, and rather than returning to the dirt, it breaks into tiny pieces which will remain on the planet forever.

In Germany, companies that produce toxic materials like plastic are forced to pay. The more lethal the chemical, the more it costs to produce. The government inspects and approves their use of chemicals, determines their recyclability, and they are given the Green Dot recycling logo. There is complete accountability.

The United States likes to operate differently, cleaning messes rather than preventing them. Our country faced difficulty when the Environmental Protection Agency was founded. They recorded all of the contaminated sites and tried to find a way to clean up. Before the EPA, no records existed and nobody knew where the toxins were buried until something happened, like the birth of a three-armed baby.

We had Superfunds, a catchy name for money used to clean a contaminated landfill. The funds were a collection of money that came from chemical companies responsible the messes. They paid into the fund in order to clean up all of the toxicity left behind from one hundred years without regulation.

Companies are no longer forced to pay for their destruction. The Superfund law expired in 1995. The companies that caused damage before the EPA don't want to be held accountable because the laws didn't exist when the committed their crimes. Since 2001, taxpayers have paid the bill. There is no funding remaining, but there are still over 40,000 toxically-contaminated landfills, known as Brownfields, in this country. 1,400 of them are considered a "national priority". In 2014, the EPA cleaned a whopping eight. They don't even make that minimal effort anymore.

It's likely there is one near you. I recently learned that the town I was raised in is a ten-minute drive from a place called Chemical Brook. It has a "Hazardous Ranking Score" of 69/100, one of the highest levels of all Brownfield sites in the country. It required $46 million to "clean up," though it's still not uncontaminated, people still have plenty of related health issues.

The entire world has known for a long time that chemicals like plastic are bad.

In 2008 alone, the United States Congress addressed over four-hundred pieces of legislation related to the production of plastic. Plastic is essentially nuclear waste, ultimately capable of causing similar effects. I remember hearing about bisphenol A (BPA) around that time, being told to avoid any plastic bottles containing the chemical. Then I was told not worry, this only seems to negatively affect women because it somehow produces artificial estrogen. That wasn't very comforting.

The real surprising fact I learned is that the harmful effects of BPA were discovered in the 1930s. It was one of the early types of plastic; quickly recognized as harmful, even cancerous. Today, there are signs on business entrances and warnings on almost every single product in California, but there are still no regulations anywhere on BPA.

The only difference between an oil spill and plastic buried in a landfill is the amount of time it takes to cause harm. Watching sea life wash up on shore with plastic stomachs allows us to see the immediate effects, the real trouble will be left to our kids. Plastic is just cooked oil.

"If the public thinks that recycling is working, then they are not going to be as concerned about the environment," Larry Thomas, former president of the Society of the Plastics Industry.

Here's a fun fact: in one year during the early 2000s, DowDupont and ExxonMobil spent $40 million "researching" recycling equipment. They spent over six times that amount, nearly $250 million, on advertising campaigns that said, "Plastics make it possible." They spent that much money on the commercials and forgot to finish their sentence. *Plastics make it possible…to steal your children's future.*

The plastics industry is allowed to produce without regulations. They have gone unchecked for decades, and we are beginning to experience the symptoms of the wastefulness. We should probably know where it ends up, it will have to be cleaned eventually.

There are plenty of ways to combat this, like the 127 countries that have bans on plastic bags. It's a very small step, and plastic bags are one of the smallest possible items. Canada has just banned all single-use plastic products, including bags, straws, six-pack rings, cutlery, and food packaging. The entire European Union will have the same ban in effect next year.

I wouldn't even know where to begin, trying to eliminate *all* plastic. There are over 90,000 different grades of plastic, and most products are made with combinations of several. Even a toothbrush often contains at least two different types of plastic. I have no desire to live without a toothbrush, but it's disappointing that we live without consideration. To recycle it, someone would be required to remove the bristles from the handle. Most recycling facilities don't even have the workforce to separate the cap from your milk jug.

I am sitting on a plastic chair, typing on a plastic keyboard, looking at a plastic laptop, under the glow of a lamp made of plastic. I am surrounded by roughly thirty plastic items at my desk, and every one of them has a different chemical recipe to produce various colors, textures, densities, etc. If I threw everything in the recycle right now, every bit of it would end in a landfill.

I would also have to pay Waste Management to use "their" landfill. Pay-as-you-throw is quite a system. It creates individual responsibility, which is great, except it alleviates the producers. In the very least, we should share the expense. Most of us really hope that our blue bins are being taken care of, but they are not. Some towns will even charge a "large item" fee, to dispose of something like a couch. I had always thought this was because they would properly dissemble and recycle the item, but the charge is simply because it takes up more space in the truck. It will end in the landfill, fully intact.

In the United States, there are over 15,000 facilities handling waste, and less than 1,000 of them are Material Recycling Facilities. These recycling facilities are generally searching for metals and cardboard, most places don't have equipment for plastic. Also, many of those facilities are incinerators, which are a short-term, poor solution. If our trash were properly separated, an incinerator might not be so bad.

Companies like Covanta just burn everything, then pay fines for the cancerous dioxins they release into the air and water. In Pittsfield, Massachusetts their incineration emissions exceeded 350% the EPA's acceptable rate. The way it is now, an incinerator is the equivalent of fracturing your skull and sticking a bandage on your nose.

This era of American society will remember plastic in the same fond way their parents remember Watergate and being lied to by the government. The way their grandparents remember the of conspiracy of DDT, by the makers and the government. Just like their great-grandparents remember being recommended a particular brand of cigarette by their dentist.

In case you youngsters weren't aware, *The Watergate Scandal* was such a big deal that every scandal after it has been given the suffix *-gate* because nobody seems to remember it was the name of the building. You may have heard of "Nipplegate" or "Gamergate" depending on your age. Really, every scandal should have -*Nixon* at the end. Nipplenixon, Tomatonixon… but I don't have time to fight that battle.

Landfillgate. Plasticgate. Foodgate. Open all of the damn gates.

Maybe after I publish, Nestle will build a little league baseball diamond for some poor community like Evart, Michigan and brag about it on *Good Morning America.*
Pacific Gas & Electric will serve pancakes in Hinkley, California. Round of applause, back to work. It's time for us to realize we're out of time, public relations and goals for the future are useless. We should have started yesterday.

The landfills are overloaded in this country, and it's the most easily correctable problem we've ever faced as a species. Every one of us is sending eight-hundred times our own weight to landfills throughout our lives. Almost all of it does not belong in the landfill, especially food and plastic. Most of us are unaware of our waste problem because it is actively being hidden. We have only been environmentally-conscious for fifty years, and our rookie mistakes are causing permanent damage. There is no room for politics on this matter, it is obvious that the Environmental Protection Agency is rendered useless by other parts of the government.

Many places have acted locally, passing restrictions within their counties or towns. I have been charged five cents for a plastic bag, though I wondered if the store paid, too. The producer obviously didn't pay. This doesn't help to solve any sort of problem, and it is baffling that we can't just say, "This was a mistake, how about we just don't use these anymore?"

Some places have tried to ban plastic bags simply because they cannot be recycled with other plastic, but they're often mixed in the blue bins. When a plastic bag enters the expensive recycling machine, it causes a jam that must be cleared by hand. Most places that make any attempt to recycle want absolutely nothing to do with a plastic bag.

The American Plastics Council ran an advertising campaign suggesting the public *"Take another look at plastics."* We did, and we realized we were right. That stuff is worse than DDT.

State and federal governments have made it difficult to act on behalf of the environment. Many states have been unable to effectively change anything. The plastics industry is often represented by the American Chemistry Council. These bottom-feeders are so skilled at government manipulation, that when Colorado, Florida and Texas tried to ban styrofoam and/or plastic bags, they cited old laws that claimed banning a container or package was illegal. It's also illegal to shower naked in Florida, but I'm sure they don't enforce that law anymore. I might be wrong.

There are still members of the government whom "deny" any climate change. As Upton Sinclair once wrote, *"It is difficult to get a man to understand something when his salary depends on not understanding it."* These politicians do not actually contest that global warming exists; they simply cannot admit this publicly because their campaigns are supported by donations. They would be out of office; their companies out of business.

In 2001, the President was Little George Bush, petroleum company owner. He appointed his friend Phillip Cooney, lawyer for the American Petroleum Institute, to his brand-new government position. *Chief of Staff in the White House Environment Office.* He had absolutely no qualification to be there, but that's how the American government works. He was caught editing EPA reports, and someone leaked them to the public. He was forced to resign, but it was no problem for him. He went to work for ExxonMobil immediately.

Another character named Michael Taylor worked for the USDA, then Monsanto, then the Food and Drug Administration. This demon helped to form American laws regarding food and pesticides for **twenty years**. None of us know his name, we definitely didn't ask him to make life or death decisions on our behalf. Why would an employee of Monsanto, the company that helped Nazis run medical tests during the Holocaust, have anything to do with the Department of Agriculture or FDA? I really thought this level of corruption only existed in comic books. No need for lobbying when you've got men on the inside.

Anyone heard from Al Gore lately? You don't stand next to petroleum manufacturers and shout about going green expecting a long career in politics. Unfortunately, they showed Mr. Gore the real *Inconvenient Truth.* They weren't about to allow him to go on spewing that hippy propaganda to the public. He made a few people lift their heads and say, "Hmmph...really?" Then they rigged the election and laughed him away; now he chases metaphorical mythical monsters in Colorado, rereading *Field Notes from A Catastrophe.*

ExxonMobil, one of the largest plastic producers in the world, "denies" any possibility of humans having an effect on the planet. Many are also Holocaust deniers, but that's a whole different topic. They say things like, *there can't be global warming, it's cold outside.* It also can't be called *global warming* anymore. We wore it out and someone hired a public relations team to invent the term "climate change." It sounds a whole lot less threatening, but we still argue about it.

"We're not destroying the world because we're clumsy. We're destroying the world because we are, in a very literal and deliberate way, at war with it."

For the sake of the public relations teams that will be attacking me on behalf of ExxonMobil, Waste Management, DowDupont, Nestle, US Foods, Sysco, Coca-Cola, Republic Services, Pepsi, Covanta, Pacific Gas & Electric, the Food Service Industry in general, and the rest that are actively and knowingly destroying your planet… We'll just get it out of the way:

My mother is a hamster, and my father smelled of elderberries. I've forgotten all about the Alamo, and I like to wear my wife's underwear on Thursday afternoons. I once told a girlfriend to make me a damn sandwich. In all fairness, she did ask, "What the fuck I want for lunch." I voted for the guy who supported the bill that caused that thing to happen, I pay for a gym membership that I never use, and it's unlikely that my obituary will say that I lit up any rooms. *If my thought-dreams could be seen, they'd probably put my head in a guillotine.*

Bob Dylan said that.

If our landfills could be seen, the people here would cry and scream.

I said that.

Cue the harmonica. Strum a chord or two.

The landfill situation won't end well; we can count on that. You can't bet your bottom dollar on the sun coming out tomorrow anymore. If you need some proof, search for some pictures of New York City right now. The streets are *filled* with garbage.

Let's move on. My secrets are out, and all that's left is the words on the page. If you're really against hamsters raising human children, you can pretend someone else wrote these words, because many people actually have. There are documentaries and books lining shelves of empty libraries everywhere. Every streaming outlet has at least ten movies on these environmental subjects.

Maybe their stories just weren't jazzy enough. My message will be delivered with your outdated cultural references and songs my *mother would know, though she was born a long, long time ago.*

These numbers are daunting, and it makes it seem an insurmountable task to correct this problem. Forty million tons of food, and three-hundred million tons of plastic into landfills per year. Truthfully, most of them are mountains rather than landfills. They smell terrible, and many things mixed into the Earth are entirely unnatural. If you bury plastic, it will stay there. If you bury food under the plastic, it won't decompose properly. It will also stay there. Then the town will build a school on it.

Everyone seems to push waste aside, comforted that someone else will take care of it. We're finally reaching the point of running out of space. It's a little overwhelming, but we're going to have lots of fun. *…A teaspoon of sugar makes the medicine go down, in the most delightful way…*

Before we take our medicine, we must take a moment to remember the words of John Muir, environmental advocate and "Father of National Parks", "*When we try to pick out anything by itself, we find it hitched to everything else in the universe.*"

Truer words have not been spoken. Each time I begin to research the amount wasted food in America, I drop down a rabbit hole of information that I wish I had never learned. I've already spent a page talking about plastic, and I've got a few more coming. I feel a responsibility to share it. I wish someone would have shared it with me, rather than stumbling across a documentary on Prime Video after scrolling for an hour in search of something to watch.

I've tried to remain on a single topic of environmental concern, but this, too, is hitched to the rest of the universe. I am forced to address all sorts of Earthly topics because each of them is pertinent to the matter at hand. Without further ado, let's dive in this landfill.

Maybe Baby, I'll Have You Someday

Each Earth Day should be considered a national holiday. Unless we're counting on a _Wall-E_ situation, in which the human race lives on spaceships in orbit; in that case, this nation has no need for Earth. Forget about it, we'll just move. _There's plenty of space, up in space!_

Fox Mulder taught me that dreams are answers to questions we haven't yet figured out how to ask. My dreams are becoming nightmares, but I figured out how to ask; here I am. This is the closest I can come to screaming from rooftops. I hope someone hears me.

I'm just a boy, standing in front of the world, asking them to love Earth.

The new Earth Day should be a worldwide celebration. I don't think it's too crazy to ask for an extension, make it Earth Week. Seven days of armistice and appreciation for life and the

Earth itself. While we celebrate this magnificent home, we're allowed the day off from work and school, the population cleans up after itself. The government could easily subsidize payments for every person with a truck and a pair of hands across the country to pitch in. It's a lot cheaper than the money we are wasting now, and they have been claiming they were going to address these problems since 1963.

We can even have corporate sponsorships and teams competing. It could be a whole bunch of fun. Give away refreshments and prizes. Whatever you've got to do. Imagine this: instead of exporting our trash, we build a new global industry that doesn't rightly exist. Start sending your trash to the U.S. because we are the world leader in waste management. We'll take your crap and make it new, or at least ensure it doesn't end up inside of the Earth. We can even sell it back to the wasteful countries as compost and energy.

I am not talking about picking up trash with those stabby ski poles on the side of the highway. I mean sorting through landfills, junkyards, and other places of waste. The trash we hide from ourselves. It's hard to believe we actually jam this waste into the Earth and call it a landfill, then build on top of it. It seems like the equivalent of sticking a pen cap in an open wound.

Nobody wants to dig through trash, but you're just leaving it for your grandchildren to clean up later. Imagine how it will smell then. It reeks already, but we can push through.

Just remember, we are trying to prevent our children from being **the first generation of Americans to grow up with a lower standard of living than their parents enjoyed.**

If we began to separate food waste today- within a few years, every farm in the United States could have zero food cost. The food which is wasted can be filtered, processed, and made into food for the billions of cows and pigs in the United States. The price of meat and dairy would drop, and the farmers would thrive. We could probably afford to feed some of the hungry human beings, too, but I'm no commie. *One step at a time, comrades.*

Seventy percent of United States land worthy of food production and involved in a growth cycle is used to feed animals, not humans. At first, you may think, *"Duh, we've got to feed all of those animals that feed us. That makes sense."*

It absolutely does not make one lick of sense. More effort and land are used to grow shit quality grain for bottom-feeding animals that we consider expendable. It's like living off of Twinkies and sleeping on the floor, because your spoiled cat will only eat filet mignon and sleep on your bed.

Whether it be grass for cows or tremendous amounts of grain for pigs and chickens, these creatures use up most of the land to be made into crappy nuggets, cheeseburgers, and hot dogs. Your barbeques could taste so much better. Your cheese, milk, everything. The better the quality of food eaten by chickens, cows and pigs, results in better meat.

Forget the grass-fed stuff. Grass-fed cows are a prime example of a bad solution to the meat industry's problems. For example, in Japan there are hundreds of different types of pork with different flavors, because the pigs are fed something specific throughout their lives. Many Americans love the flavor of applewood smoked bacon, but they would be blown away eating pork that was from a pig that ate nothing but discarded apples from the local orchard.

A cow *will* eat grass, if that's all that is provided. In total desperation, a human might do the same. Cows have something like

20,000 taste buds. Humans have around 10,000; and even the most extreme vegan doesn't eat grass because it's gross.

The space required is actually a problem of its own, because 80% of the deforestation in the Amazon has happened only to fill 25% of the world's demand for beef. The cows require massive amounts of land to chew this grass and defecate all day- in the same field. Animals raised for slaughter produce 130 times as much waste as the entire human population. Our waste is chemically treated in sanitation plants, but animal waste is not: Typically, it is sprayed onto land, then much of it runs off to pollute groundwater or streams. Manure good; sewage bad. Then we eat this meat- composed of their grassy manure diet. That is, if you buy grass-fed. Yum. Most of us can't afford to live like the elite and buy organic food, so it's even worse for us. They are fed grain and other unsatisfying nonsense. It's so useless they just call it "feed." As a result, meat tastes bland, which is why we smother it in cheese and sauces.

How about we give them our half-eaten dinners and apple cores, even that bag of spring mix that sits in your crisper until it expires and feels like it came pre-mixed with Italian dressing. The cows wouldn't mind one bit.

To produce **one pound** of beef, it requires 2,400 gallons of water and 12 pounds of grain. A good-sized steer produces 430 pounds of beef between all of the various cuts. That is 1,032,000 gallons of water and 5,160 pounds of grain per cow. The five thousand may seem light, but you need to visualize the plant it comes from. Imagine how much space that grain requires. Over their life, a cow is easily consuming a field's worth.

Controlling the waste is a highly profitable opportunity, charging businesses to take care of their food waste in the same way as trash companies. Then it can be processed and sold to a farm. I'm not an expert in business, but it sounds to me like two chances to make money off of the leftovers on a table. You'd be a walrus with two carpenters, looks like lots of oysters.

I know it is a bit absurd of me to ask the corporations to halt production and begin making money in different ways. It is as simple as this: You have had a hand in destroying the planet, and now it will require two hands to clean it up. Money and profit will not to suffer. More importantly, neither will your children. Unless you act now, all the little heirs of your fortunes will have no planet over which to rule, and the companies you built will fall. It may not be your children or grandchildren, but the great grandkids will undoubtedly be living in a world much uglier than this one.

The governments have not helped, and their miniscule efforts barely register as having any effect. We cannot depend on politicians for all of the effort to be made, or to only be willing to adjust our behavior because a law is passed. It's been fifty years since that Earth Day, and during that time the problem has actually become worse. According to the National Waste and Recycling Association:

Americans generated 258 million tons of waste in 2014, nearly triple the amount from 1960, and 169 million tons of that ended up in landfills and incinerators. The U.S. has the highest amount of waste generated per person of any country at an average of 4.6 pounds per day. In a lifetime, the average American will discard nearly 800 times the amount of his or her adult weight.

The best part of the government equation is that they actively stand in the way of simple progresses. When the whistle is blown, and companies have been called out for their environmental abominations, they are enabled to hide behind the government and its laws. "We follow every rule and regulation laid forth by *[insert local, state, or federal government]*", the worst part being that this is actually true. Don't forget, these politicians are meant to represent us, that is their purpose for existing. Their original purpose, anyways. It hasn't always been like *Real Housewives* on the hill. Well, it probably has but we weren't all actively watching.

Following every law actually allows this endangerment of humanity to occur and the government does nothing but *react* to the disasters caused. It requires *Erin Brokovich*, and then Julia Roberts pretending to be Erin Brokovich, to make a few people understand a serious problem exists. The corporation paid a settlement, after years of begging. Roberts won best actress and the movie made $256 million at the box-office.

The guilty party, Pacific Gas & Electric, paid out $333 million to the citizens of Hinkley, California. A small fraction of their annual earnings. $333 million to a corporation like PG&E is equivalent to maybe fifty cents to you or me. They said they're sorry and moved on with their lives.

I can't even guarantee that they said they were sorry. Don't quote me on that.

In case you missed it, in the 50s and 60s, PG&E dumped about 370 million gallons of chromium-tainted wastewater into unlined ponds. Residents in the area developed a great deal of health problems, including many developing Hodgkin's Lymphoma. It took a lawyer on a warpath, millions of dollars, and lots of suffering to even get the giant corporation to acknowledge the problem existed. The town was gutted by Pacific Gas and Electric, and they tried to hide from that fact for a long time. They were successful, too. Then Hollywood made a movie about it.

Pacific Gas & Electric, the evil corporate protagonist of *Erin Brokovich,* remains one of the largest corporations in California, providing services to 16 million people- I even paid them for electricity while living in San Diego County.

In addition to their rape of Hinkley, they have also caused a number of wildfires and other natural disasters. They're carrying on just fine. Business never suffered. People sure did though. This was even before 2010, when the government declared that corporations are people.

I happened to live in Hinkley, don't ask me why. It is a ghost town, full of boarded up homes and destitute structures that may or may not have been homes. The water is not safe for drinking, cooking, or bathing. Some citizens have spent thousands of dollars on devices which supposedly filter the damaging ingredient known as chromium-6 in the water. It still smells like something weird afterwards, and most choose the safe route, avoiding it entirely.

While I was there, one man in town was issued a fine for selling his vegetables at a local market, when it had been discovered that they were grown in Hinkley's soil with PG&E-infused water. My landlord even offered me some vegetables from his personal garden, convinced that the water would not affect the plants. This was some interesting logic to me, but I flatly refused. I don't really need a third ear growing on my forehead.

The temperature in Hinkley remains steadily above 100 degrees during the summer, all day long. The sun is beaming down by ten a.m. at full force. The air is dry, and once a week, the desert winds are so intense that warnings are issued. The living conditions are far less than favorable. It sits ten miles outside of Barstow, one of the final tourist destinations on Route 66 in California, if you're heading for the West Coast.

The population gathers its water supply from the nearby Wal-Mart in Barstow. The town of Hinkley is effectively dead, and it is a seriously depressing place to live. The house around the corner was boarded up, and the boards read "FUCK PG&E" though someone clearly tried to cover that up. A security team surveys the town 24-hours a day, to ensure that squatters do not take refuge in the empty houses. It's just a few guys driving around in trucks, but their presence is annoying.

Hinkley appears to be the location of a great battle with bombs and napalm, like a scene from a post-apocalyptic movie of some kind, and not in a cool way. I think I may have seen Sarah Conner's skeleton stuck on a fence at the edge of town.

If shown a photo of Hinkley, most of the American population would not believe that this place is in California, let alone in the United States. Even the producers of *Erin Brokovich* didn't want to look at it. They filmed the movie outside of Hinkley and in Los Angeles.

Wouldn't it be nice to *prevent* the disaster? Is this some sort of collective fear of missing out? While I think it would be quite fun to live in a post-apocalyptic world, I see no reason to create one. The characters in the books and movies always seem to miss the past, which I suppose would be, right freaking now.

Earth Day and the blue bins with three little arrows have become a symbol of an effort made, and an effort largely wasted. Reduce, reuse, recycle, yadda, yadda. The recycling industry should be a booming battle of titans, competing with their counterparts in production. Instead, it is an unorganized offering of an empty promise unfulfilled.

Imagine, a corporation that people liked having around! There should be a Microsoft-Apple type of celebrity in recycling. *The Wolf of Every Street.* The Elon Musk or Mark Cuban of waste. That would a rich guy I would gladly support. We probably cannot count on Mr. Musk saving us here, he's headed for Mars. Though he could increase his worth by creating a real way to take care of all the leftover plastic after we ban the stuff…

To add insult to this planetary injury, most of the stuff going in blue bins doesn't even end up being recycled. Less than 10%, actually. The people who make plastic were allowed to determine how recycling works. The local recycling plant doesn't even have the chemicals to break down most of your plastics. Those little numbers on the bottom of your blueberries means absolutely nothing, except for varying chemicals. The numbers were invented in 1988 by the Society of Plastics. DowDupont had done it again. They convinced the government DDT was good, and then they did it again with plastic. It's like cancer, there may be some that are more malignant than others, but it's still cancer.

Companies like Nestle make claims to be "100% recyclable by 2025." Coca-Cola promised 25%, they even released something called the Plant Bottle. They replaced a small fraction of plastic with sugarcane. It's still made of plastic, but it says *plant* in the name, so everyone had better stop complaining. Nobody wanted to mention that they abandoned their glass bottles in 1973 for absolutely no reason.

These statements are 100% unadulterated propaganda, an evil and heartless fucking lie to continue selling plastic. They have done it before, and if left unchecked, they will do it again.

Of the 72 billion water bottles produced annually, 55 million will go to landfills. The other 17 million *may* be "downcycled" into a rug or a t-shirt, however, either product would be poor quality and quickly make their way to a landfill. Those 17 million plastic bottles just had an extra year of shitty life before the dump. This is absolutely not what the public believes recycling to be. I thought the idea was to completely avoid the landfill.

Until two years ago, China was taking over 70% of our plastic. It was a simple way to push everything away from our land. They have completely banned the import of plastic because most of what was sent there was useless. It piled up so badly that they had to defend themselves, enacting a "National Sword" policy. We have not felt the repercussions yet, but we are only two years into what will be ecological disaster. They weren't just collecting from the United States either, it was more than half of the plastic in the world. Plastic production has not decreased, in fact there are several new types of plastic that have come to market since then. The whole world is, quite simply, fucked.

I remember hearing all about fracking around 2013, and hearing of many worldwide protests related to the practice. Fracking is a simple process, in which oil companies blast water into the ground to "fracture" the Earth and force the black gold from within. It's terrible for every aspect of the environment- land, air, and water. Apparently, this process is the main method of gathering petroleum for plastics. Since 2010, fracking projects have dramatically increased, with 334 separate United States locations being fracked for roughly $200 billion worth of oil. In 2019 alone, ExxonMobil, BASF, and Shell have also announced hundreds of billions of dollars invested in new petroleum plants.

In 2007, people made a fuss about plastic for a few weeks. Nestle responded by making the size of the caps smaller and thinning out the bottles. They bragged about it on their packaging. I remember it vividly; I was in high school at the time. Every day almost all students came to class with a Nestle-Poland Spring water bottle which sat at the front of their desk. We had perfectly functional water fountains, but I guess those weren't cool.

The week that Nestle released these new "eco-friendly" plastic water bottles, they rolled off of desks all day long because the bottle was too weak to support its contents. Hooray for conservation. There is no such thing as "eco-friendly plastic" but we all stopped whining, so they had averted their problem. Their sentiment about environmentally cautious chemicals equates to a rapist demanding a lesser sentence because he was passionate and looked the victim in the eyes.

Companies like Nestle, ExxonMobil, and DowDupont are rapists of the Earth, and they're looking you right in the eye. ...*the kind of guys that would fuck a person in the ass and not even have the goddam common courtesy to give him a reach-around.*

Oh, is rape an extreme analogy? It's not an analogy at all. They are literally raping the Earth. They are scum-sucking, soul-devouring liars, and that is a nice way to phrase it.

If I grab someone and penetrate them until liquid comes out, what would you call that? Ever seen thousands of oil pumpjacks thrusting up and down in the plains of Texas, bleeding her dry? Didn't you see British Petroleum dump its load on Louisiana? They didn't walk right for years.

I may have just lost all of my sensitive readers. They can suck a plastic bottle.

George Clinton and P-Funk already said it in 1971. Nobody listened. Let's hear it again, cue Eddie Hazel on guitar.

Mother Earth is pregnant for the third time, for y'all have knocked her up
I have tasted the maggots in the mind of the universe, I was not offended
For I knew I had to rise above it all, or drown in my own shit

Amen.

For those who still feel like I'm just a pervert being too extreme, consider this:

Law and Order: Special Victims Unit is about to reach 500 episodes after twenty-one years on the air. Mariska Hargitay is raking in $450,000 per episode. The USA Channel exists almost entirely to air its reruns. If you're living under a rock, the show depicts an entity of the NYPD that handles cases which are sexually related, the Special Victims Unit.

The public can't seem to watch enough of it, some of the worst crimes in our society. I've personally seen every episode of the first twelve seasons. While I love Olivia, Munch, and Fin- I just couldn't watch without Stabler. *Special Victims Unit* may be on the air forever, though.

The Earth is the most Special Victim there ever was, and ever will be. Unless we colonize Mars, hopefully that never happens. We'd bend that planet over and fuck it, too.

I was there when *Fifty Shades of Grey* sold 125 million copies worldwide, followed by its corresponding film trilogy which made $1 billion at the box-office. I will never forget discovering a copy on my supervisor's desk; a 56-year-old church-goer who once exclaimed, "Oh, sugar!" and apologized for cussing.

Society can't pretend to be prude now. Sex sells, and for anyone not buying, they'll be angry enough to talk about it. Maybe even write a tweet. At least one more human being will be aware of the problem.

Anyone in the plastic industry will tell you flatly it is exponentially more affordable to make new plastic, than it is to "recycle" it. In the same way that many restaurants and businesses don't use recycle bins because it's far more affordable to fill a dumpster. In fact, even if the business were to fill their dumpster twice in a single week and pay for an extra trash pickup, it would *still be cheaper* than sorting it and "recycling."

Are we beginning to understand how the problem is just moved around from place to place and never properly handled?

Most importantly, even if the effort were made, plastic can only be recycled once or twice because it degrades in the process. Then it must be burned or dumped, but even burning it can be expensive and have negative environmental effects. **No matter what, plastic will ultimately occupy space in the ocean or a landfill.** This seems like a thought that is so distant from our minds, and very well might be a fundamental issue.

There is one important thing that we must understand, living in this modern world. Not too long ago, before the age of plastic, it would have been perfectly fine to throw your trash in the ocean. It hardly would have made much difference at all, maybe annoyed a few sea creatures. This is what was done for thousands of years by any society with access to water. If they weren't near water, they just threw it in the street, which led to the Black Plague. Similarly, if they had landfills, it would have been fine. No plastic.

The difference was that all of their trash was made of natural materials. I'm sure it's no fun for the sea life, but anything thrown in the ocean would have deteriorated. We now live in a world with unnatural chemicals, and plastic in oceans and landfills is a serious problem.

Before diving into this research topic, I had never really considered the "life" of a piece of plastic. There's no way I am alone. I would have to admit that there was a flitter of an idea in my mind that plastic could be used infinitely, like metals. If it wasn't "downcycled" into a new t-shirt, it must be made into *something*, right? Everything is made of plastic these days.

I've known vegan girls that made their own kombucha and tapped Maple trees. Environmental warriors that make their own deodorant and take it as a compliment when someone shouts, "Take a shower, you dirty hippy!"

I've been on a romantic moonlight stroll in Oregon, somehow finding myself help my date sort through a garbage bin full of recyclables. She just couldn't leave it that way; it wasn't who she was, and I respected that no matter how much I moaned and groaned. At least somebody around here stands for *something*. I doubt we would have stopped if she had known that recycling is a boogie monster.

No one ever mentioned anywhere that the recycling process is just a delay from the landfill. The truth is, **there really is no such thing as recycling.** Let that soak in. Am I repeating myself? Good.

It's hard not to write a *War and Peace* sized novel about plastic, but **food waste** requires a fraction of the effort to battle. Almost no effort at all, actually. The benefits are immeasurable. We don't even have to battle corporations. The amount of food waste in the world is inconceivable. Did I mention it's eighty billion pounds per year? In just FOOD.

The United States is the worst perpetrator, given its level of comfort and ease of access. Food is cheaper in the U.S. than anywhere in the world. This is largely due to government subsidies on soda, corn, wheat, milk, and soybeans, amongst a few other things. This funding allows the farmers to cover some operation costs and sell to consumers for an affordable price. It's also the reason that a 2-liter of Mountain Dew is cheaper than a bottle of

Dasani, despite the fact that both are Pepsi products and the more expensive one is tap water.

These silly policies often waste large amounts of farmland, because it is totally absurd for a farm to exist for one crop. Soil functions best when rotated, and many crops actually benefit from other plants growing in the same field. A farm should grow several crops and the land should be continuously full, even the most amateur gardener knows of soil systems. The farmers probably know too, but the government won't give them their money if they plant carrots after harvesting the tomatoes. It's better to be wasteful.

There's no reason for wasting any food. A person who wastes food should be viewed in the same regard as a litterbug.

I have lived in the United States my entire life, and people are always claiming it's the best country in the world. Well, that remains to be proven. Right now, we are last in the standings in the most important match that has ever been played.

This is the Olympics, the Super Bowl, all of those horse races, the World Series, and the Stanley Cup rolled into one. If necessary, get patriotic about it. Your sense of pride for the land of the free and the home of the brave will be forever remembered by its tremendous amount of trash- most of which was food that we just didn't eat. Otherwise, the lyrics really need to be "land*fill* of the free…" and I don't mean that insultingly. I'm just a stickler for lyrical accuracy.

Even think of the simple fact that your trash bin will no longer smell like decomposing food. Keep a container outside and your trash bag will last an extra week or two. That could be enough motivation to separate food waste or compost, right there.

Let's try to avoid plastic containers- it's ironic that in response to an uproar about plastic production, they produced a whole bunch of plastic bins to collect the plastic. That's not rain on your wedding day, Alanis Morissette ironic- that's hardcore sardonicism. It's only the first chapter, somebody get those not-plastic food bins in production before the others finish reading.

The wonderfully terrible fact is that every single person on the planet is guilty. This is the only social, economic, and political battle that involves every single human being that eats food to survive. That's all of us. A third of the food produced globally is wasted. There is no escaping or excusing. It is rare to find a cause which has <u>absolutely no reason</u> to make an argument.

Even if you believe the Earth is flat, this is your problem. In fact, if you're right, the flat-Earth would fill up faster than a globe. I'll leave that subject alone.

It doesn't matter if you're an anti-vaxxer, anti-masker, or anti-dentite.

We are all responsible, and unless you're a member of the Church of Euthanasia, you want this planet to continue having humans live upon its surface. I think that even they will be on board with this newly recognized battle, I'll have to find out at my first sermon.

The following story involves a small cast of characters, who sought to change the world, beginning with their own local environment. The world they were forced to interact with on a daily basis. They didn't ask the government for its help; the rippling effect took care of that.

They didn't write to their congressman or wave signs on the street. They very simply held up a mirror to society and reminded them of one thing. When you throw away, there is no place for it to go- it simply waits for the future. For our waste, away is not a place, but a time.

The Great Procrastination of Humanity. The Screaming Spring.

In environmental justice, the people are supposedly represented by two separate yet equally important groups: the elected government, who make laws, and the Environmental Protection Agency, who clean up our messes. Dun- dun.

All of the events relating to restaurant experiences are real and took place in a wide variety of eateries over the course of the past fifteen years.

All of the statistics and facts have been collected from data provided by the United States government, environmental organizations, and the food, waste, and plastic industries. More importantly, almost all of this information is available on any streaming service, every magazine still in publication, and in hundreds of books.

My sources are included at the end.

The events relating to our three characters won't take place until tomorrow.

All of the waste is ours.

This page is for you to tear from the book.

I don't care if you're in a library. I apologize for being old. I meant to say, screenshot it on your device. Post it on all media outlets. If you are actually in a library, good for you. However, if you are reading this page- please follow the instructions because clearly someone who visited your library did not.

Bring it to your grocery store or favorite restaurant. Pass it around your workplace or school. Hang it in the town square. There is possible repercussion for giving edible, unused food to another person. There is actually a law encouraging you to give that food to someone who needs it.

THE FEDERAL BILL EMERSON GOOD SAMARITAN DONATION ACT WAS ENACTED IN 1996 BY PRESIDENT BILL CLINTON.

Its purpose: To encourage the donation of food and grocery products to nonprofit organizations for distribution to needy individuals by giving the Model Good Samaritan Food Donation Act the full force and effect of law.

The Bill Emerson Good Samaritan Food Donation Act

* The Federal Bill Emerson Good Samaritan Food Donation Act protects the donor and the recipient agency against liability, excepting only gross negligence and/or intentional misconduct. In addition, each state has passed Good Samaritan Laws that provide liability protection to good faith donors.

The Cook

Tiger got to hunt; bird got to fly,

Man got to sit and wonder; why, why, why?

Tiger got to sleep; bird got to land;

Man got to tell himself he understand.

-Kurt Vonnegut- *Cat's Cradle*

Another day in the life of your everyday citizen. Pay rate just enough above minimum wage to keep me placated; a crappy apartment that allows every sound from the neighbor through the walls; and a cabinet full of ramen noodles. A junk-pile car that runs, most of the time. Bills that never seem to add up or balance out. Some lumpy three-year-old department store bed that never allows me to sleep through the night. Like most weekends, I'm exhausted and ready for the day to end before I've even moved from bed.

Every Saturday morning I find myself fighting the sun for some sleep, despite it being ten minutes until my shift begins. The restaurant didn't even close until 12:30 last night, then closing duties lasted until about 3:00 am, and by the time I fell asleep the sun was rising.

Back to the grind at 11:00 am for what we call the "clopen" shift. Close the restaurant and the return immediately in the morning to open it again. It's especially terrible after a late close like last night. As usual, the closing shift ran until the early morning for some uninteresting reason. Someone called out; a table of ten arrived right before close; some extraneous task given by the manager. *"Can you clean the wall behind the sauce station?"*

Oh, yes please! I just stood here for an hour with no orders, doing nothing; why not add an extra task to prevent me from going home before the sun comes up?

I thought I would be out of the restaurant industry after graduating with a bachelor's degree. It hardly seemed possible to accumulate such debt and continue working the same old job, but I was desperate. I hadn't made the most effort to start a career, but I expected, in the least, to work in something that resembled my field of study.

The summer after graduation seemed to be full of promise, declaring myself retired from the wondrous culinary world. I said I would never cook for anyone else again. I began working at an insurance firm, of course, because I had obtained a degree in Marine Biology. I even applied to the City Aquarium, which told me I was overqualified for the janitor position and underqualified to care for the animals.

Insurance was the obvious next step in the progression to becoming the next Jacques Cousteau- making baseless calls to uninterested people and trying to persuade them that their coverage was not good enough.

I was told that each employee usually made lots of money on commission; but after three months, the realization came- this was a manipulative impossibility. I was earning no more than in the restaurant; and I had traded in the physical tolls for a dose of serious mental abuse. Screen gazing at an office job is a surefire way to lose your mind; and I began to understand this society's behavior a bit more.

Once again, doing this same rigmarole at another restaurant. Climb past thirty boxes delivered this morning. Not a good sign- they're usually in the fridge, but today the driver came before the manager. Here we go. Clock in, wash up, grab an apron, and turn on all of the appliances. Gather the soups and sauces for the steamtable and get them heating on the grill. Nacho cheese, soups, chili, butter, and the buffalo dip… looks funny.

The buffalo dip is a processed mixture of shredded chicken and something like cheese. Looks like it's in the same pan I had used on Friday- the one with the bent corner that won't sit right. It looked like someone had changed it on Thursday night, so on Friday morning, I just added another bag and mixed it in.

It is an expected standard in kitchens to label and date a container, so that there is no question of quality. The cooks shouldn't be sniffing things and asking if it's okay to serve. There are suggested amounts of time for each type of ingredient to last while sitting out on the serving line.

It also helps to keep track of food- if something got pushed to the back of the fridge, I can check the label and know when it was made. Health Inspectors will fail a restaurant for improper labeling. Most restaurants respond by placing meaningless stickers on them, just in case an inspection takes place.

In at least five restaurants I have worked, the process for dating and labeling is quite a deceitful spectacle. If I am working on Wednesday, the containers have Wednesday stickers on them. Not because everything was freshly prepared on this day, but quite simply because it is Wednesday. The night before, someone had taken the food that was out all day, emptied it into a new container and labeled it Wednesday.

At the end of dinner of Wednesday, unless it looks totally inedible, I will empty the stuff into a new container and label it Thursday. This will carry on until the food is gone or appears to have spoiled. I have been "trained" to do this by different general managers, even a chef that had recently finished culinary school.

It's Monday, and if use of this pan began on Thursday; that means this container holding buffalo dip is four or five days old. What has remained in the bottom has been stirred up again and again, mixed right in. It has been placed on the grill, heated to 350 degrees, and then placed in a steam-table- a container which holds things that need to be kept warm, like nacho cheese, chili, chili, soups, etc.- remaining there for the entire eleven hours of operation.

During lunch, the container ran low and another bag was added. The bottom was stirred in again. I clock out before the dinner rush begins, and the new staff comes in, welcomed by an early dinner rush that keeps steady through the night.

At the end of the night, the container wasn't changed. They had only scheduled two people to close, and the place filled up thirty minutes beforehand. All the crew could do was cover the pans, there was certainly no time to create a whole sink full of dishes. The buffalo dip from last Thursday lives on.

Tuesday morning, a different person opened the restaurant. The container was placed on the grill, heated to 350 degrees, and then placed in a steamtable for the entire eleven hours of operation. The shredded chicken and processed cheese being scooped upon your nachos may very well be two weeks old, depending on who was working.

I'm not even sure if it actually started on Thursday, that was a guess. When I return, Wednesday of the next week, I notice the buffalo dip is still in the pan with the bent corner. It can't possibly be the same batch, can it?

Oh yes, it can. When I push hard with the ladle, a charred chunk of black scum arises from the bottom. I empty the container into the trash, despite the fact that the pan is full. I can't serve any of this, and it probably shouldn't have been served the past four days.

At the bottom of the pan is two inches of crusty chicken and processed cheese from the week before. If I hadn't forced the ladle into the mixture and broke the encrusted bottom layer, it would have remained there throughout the day. I left the pan to soak, but it was so disgusting and solid that the dishwasher just threw the pan in the trash. *Did you miss that new episode of The Bachelor because you were on the toilet after dinner?*

This isn't some dramatization, this is the type of thing happening in restaurants, hospitals, schools, and grocery store eateries across the country. It's not a malicious attempt by the cook to sabotage your health. It's not even negligence. It's a symptom of a system, in which a crew of poorly paid workers are given the responsibility to act like your mother, cooking and serving you food.

It's their job, and most of them are not paid well. Every day they repeat the same chores with the same ingredients in mass amounts, which is disgusting most of the time. Ever looked at five gallons of tuna fish "salad"? For the record, this is not a salad in any way, shape, or form- it is dead fish smothered in mayonnaise.

Try making the shit on a daily basis. Slapping a gallon of mayonnaise in a gigantic bowl of a chopped blunderbuss of fish parts. It doesn't even really appear to all be tuna, but we won't speculate.

The tuna salad is usually mixed by hand, because it would be really difficult to do it any other way. If you simply put gloves on, there is no need for a utensil. When mixing in a large bowl, you must make sure not to sink your hands beyond the wrist, where the glove ends.

With a big batch, it becomes messy as it nears completion. The gloves are covered in dead fish and mayonnaise, and they're hard to maneuver. It usually requires two pairs to make a food-service sized pile of tuna fish salad. Behind the scenes, the prep cooks usually wear gloves. There are some things that should not be done without gloves, like preparing meat. I have seen some disgusting things.

Chefs do not wear gloves while cooking, it makes cooking far more difficult. They melt when hot and nearly everything in the kitchen involves heat. Gloves can also seriously increase the risk of cross-contamination. Most cooks remain sanitary by just paying attention to what they touch and washing their hands frequently. The gloves are extremely annoying, and most of them are covered in powder which gets everywhere.

I used to work with a really nice prep guy, we worked many shifts together. There was a language barrier that prevented us from knowing each other beyond greetings, but it never caused any problems. I looked forward to working with him because he worked his ass off and hardly said a word. Peaceful.

He had some terrible habits, and each time I tried to say something about it, I would find myself giving up. One of these habits was never wearing gloves, no matter what. I later found out he was allergic to the powder in the gloves. He washed his hands plenty and was very neat, but with his bare hands he would handle raw chicken and ground beef.

This man was of Eastern European descent, and his dark features were coated in hair thicker than a cashmere sweater. Popping out by his neck, on the back of his hands, everywhere. The guy at the beach that makes you feel terrible because you subconsciously did a double-take. *Is that a sweater?*

He made the tuna salad almost every day with no gloves. Most of the time it was done before I arrived, but when I happened to see it, I would shudder. Just reaching right in, up to his hairy elbows and squeezing the stuff between his gorilla fingers to mix well. At the end, he grabs it by the handful and pans it up, to be served at lunch.

I'll just provide a few more things I have seen in the restaurants I worked, to paint a better picture of the millions of ways your food is probably being unintentionally mishandled.

Working in a grocery store, the most popularly selling item was rotisserie chicken. The place at was a small California chain competing with Whole Foods- mostly organic, expensive, and niche items. Everything was farm fresh and it was a nice place to work. I only include these details because despite it being such a nice place, the rotisserie chicken process always disturbed me. I don't even want to imagine what goes on at Wal-Mart.

Every single day, we sold about fifty rotisserie chickens. If you want to cook a quality chicken, you let it sit in *brine*, a water mixture of salt and spices, for some time before it is cooked. Fifty chickens per day requires a big container with a lot of brine. We used two fifty-gallon trashcans on wheels, and filled them up with a hose.

The hose rested on the ground at all times, under a sink in the back corner. I was always sure to stand and hold the hose, ensuring that the dirty thing didn't touch the inside of the container. Every other employee dropped the filthy hose in the bucket and left it to fill.

These trashcans were refilled with raw chicken every single day, always being utilized because they sell out consistently. The brine was changed every three days, and by the end it was a 50-gallon bucket filled with several days-worth of briny chicken blood.

Employees do not work every single day, and there are multiple. The container was hardly ever dated. There were plenty of times the brine lasted for at least a week, and I never saw these raw-chicken buckets washed. There was no chance to do so, we always needed to be brining more chicken. Empty it out, fill it back up, and toss more chickens in there.

Preparing chicken is always gross, especially when you're forced to deal with it in large amounts. Those creatures are gross even when they're alive. I've seen chickens eat cat shit and search for a second helping.

This is partly why chicken tastes best fried, and restaurants serving their wings are extremely popular. I had the privilege of working at one of them which featured large breasts. In these places-the menu is primarily composed of different fried chicken and appetizers. We had five fryolators, two intended for fries and appetizers, one for seafood, and the rest were constantly full of chicken wings.

Breaded wings leave flour behind, which cause the fry oil to be filtered or changed daily. During a real busy day, it may be done after lunch. It is easy to tell the quality of the oil, because it begins as a transparent yellow and turns black when used thoroughly. There are also testing strips in the kitchen, but expired oil will also generate smoke, the clear indicator that stuff has to go. In the dining room, you can tell by the color of your fried food. The darker it is, the older the oil.

The filtering/changing process of the oil takes a long time. When possible, it is started before close, so that it doesn't keep employees there for hours. They must be turned off in order to filter, so we do them one at a time, in case we get hit with business. Turn one off, clean it, and turn it back on. Go to the next one.

During eight months of employment, the seafood fryolator was never changed. It was the only one dedicated to seafood, so it had to remain on throughout the night. When close comes around, the rest of the fryolators are filtered and ready for tomorrow, nobody wants to go back for one more.

The same fry oil cooked at least 500 pieces of fried cod and at least 1,000 shrimp. It won't harm you, remaining steadily at 350 degrees, but it sure doesn't add flavor. The oil was completely black. Whatever, just smother it in butter or tartar sauce.

Even the most observant manager cannot monitor the daily decisions of all of the employees. Many of them try, the micromanagement in food service is overwhelming. It is almost always misdirected. There is still plenty of room for lots to go wrong in a kitchen, and it usually does.

The most important resource in a kitchen is towels or rags. Each restaurant has a service which picks up their dirty towels each week and drops off a load of clean ones. The companies provide linen bags for pickup.

Despite my objections, the dirty linen bag was always hung from the side of the drying rack, where clean dishes are stored. Cooks would throw dirty rags toward it, most often missing. We would just collect them up from the floor and put them in the bag at the end.

I noticed someone had thrown a soapy rag soaked in chicken blood and missed, leaving it dangling from a shelf on the rack. On the bottom shelf was a pot, which we used almost exclusively to make clam chowder. The rag had dripped continuously into the pot for a few hours.

I was in the middle of ten things, and I completely forgot what I had seen almost immediately. Five minutes later, that raw chicken blood became the foundation for the day's "New England Clam Chowder," though the clams weren't fresh and it had no bacon, so it wasn't really New England style. Anyways, he didn't look inside, he just grabbed the pot and poured in the cream.

In another restaurant, we had apparently run out of rags during dinner. Not only does that suck for cooking, but think about cleaning the kitchen without towels the end of the night. Before we had even reached that point, I noticed dishwasher lifting up his shirt and using the inside of it to dry plates. I told him to stop doing that and allow them to air-dry. He had already been utilizing this method for two hours and half of the dinner I had just served was on those plates.

If the mere mention of this isn't gross enough- consider the fact that he was severely overweight, sweat excessively, and he was nearing the end of a double shift. To add a little cherry on top- this dishwasher used to eat leftovers from plates. The waitresses would bring trays back with half-eaten burgers, fries, whatever wasn't consumed in the dining room. His favorite was mashed potatoes, which he often scooped directly with his dirty dishwashing hands. It was quite disgusting to see.

Before anyone tries to defend this man and claim he may have had no other way to eat, I can assure you this was not true. He was in his mid-20s, living at home with his well-to-do parents. He drove to work in his father's second car, a three-year old BMW. He was just stoned, hungry, and disgusting. The restaurant didn't feed him, though, and to some extent I understand his hunger. He just took it to a whole different level. Working around food makes you hungry constantly, even when you have seen the terrible possibilities of that very same food.

While sorting through a shipment of beef at a barbeque joint, I found a small eyeball within some beef, which employees guessed to belong to a mouse or rabbit. If you're not aware, cows are herbivores and do not eat mice or rabbits. The beef around the eyeball was removed, the rest went into chili.

I have seen a decomposing mouse in a box of pork rinds, as if eating the fried skin of a pig weren't gross enough on its own. I found that mouse at the bottom of the pork rinds, after the entire container had been served. This was different from the eyeball in the beef, because there was no wondering if digestion may have been involved. The mouse had clearly entered the box during storage, had a feast, and died. I don't know how long it takes for a dead mouse to decompose, but this thing had to have been dead in the box for a while. Whoops.

The average citizen who dines regularly at common restaurants can only be living by two possible philosophies. There may be outliers, but this is pretty cut and dry.

The first type of person has absolutely no idea what is happening behind the scenes. They've never seen *Kitchen Nightmares*. By some stroke of magnificent stupidity, they expect the bro making minimum wage to give a fuck about their crappy frozen meal. Not to mention, that ball-scratchin' bro just made that same exact slop of shit for twenty other lazy customers that just didn't want to cook tonight, or worse, didn't have the capability.

It may seem unlikely but the amount of business; time spent waiting food; the number of complaints; dependence upon restaurant food, and the utter disregard for those involved with producing it- has led me to believe that this uninformed portion of the demographic equals roughly half of the customers.

The other half is aware of the horrors and creates cognitive dissonance between their mouths and their eyes. Despite watching Chef Ramsay ask for sick bags, pull cockroaches from refrigerators, or gag as he sniffs green beef; the majority still find themselves ordering out the next day. *That can't possibly be what my favorite restaurant is like.* No way. Regardless, after a long day of work, the joy of cooking ain't all that joyful. Just fill me up and plop me on the couch. *Quickly, please.*

If you live in the United States, all you can hope for is a Health Inspectors sign in the window- which hardly means anything. *Don't worry, there's a piece of paper with a red "B" from last June on the door, must be good.* The last time I saw a health inspector, he was in the kitchen for five minutes. He opened one refrigerator and said, "Looks good to me, I've got Sox tickets tonight!"

There are ninety-two episodes of the U.S. version of *Kitchen Nightmares*. There are over 650,000 restaurants in the United States. Chef Ramsay didn't visit them all, and I guarantee that if he did, he would close 450,000 of those places.

Maybe these people think that because it's a TV show, it must be staged. These restaurants must be the most extreme examples, that's why it's on television. Every other Subway and local Mom and Pop restaurant are spotless, and the food quality is top rate.

A great deal of variables caused this society's dependence upon restaurants, ranging from the availability of ingredients and their prices, to a person's ability to cook, but the most important factor is laziness. *Sorry, not sorry.* There are many obstacles preventing most of us from making quality food at home, but most of them can be boiled down to excuses. It's almost always more affordable, and you can cook whatever you please by simply finding one of the billions of recipes available online.

Go shopping and cook a recipe. It may just blow your mind, and it won't be as hard or time-consuming as you think. Watch *MasterChef* instead of *Kitchen Nightmares* and learn something. The microwave is meant to reheat food, it should never be used to cook the food. In many restaurants across this country, the microwave is used far more than any other appliance in the kitchen. If you are not currently living in a college dorm, you should not be eating microwaved food.

If only most of the consumers knew that almost all of American restaurant food comes from less than ten companies, and the rest of the food is the same exact thing you can buy in the supermarket- thawed, and portioned. Then handed to you. If only they knew. Almost everything is prepared and boxed over one year before it ships to a restaurant, in the meantime it is stored in a massive Midwestern warehouse.

I have worked in restaurants in Massachusetts, Maine, California, and Oregon. Fine dining, pizza joints, coffee shops, schools, industrial cafes, family-style restaurants, country clubs- all varieties of eateries. Every single week, each of the 20-plus restaurants I worked at has most of the ingredients delivered by companies like Sysco International, US Foods, or Performance Food Service. Sometimes, *all* of the ingredients for a restaurant arrive on these 18-wheelers from industrial warehouses in middle America.

Every single restaurant where I was employed was provided at least one item by Sysco, in particular. The same exact frozen foods and ingredients to make almost every recipe at every restaurant in the country.

Working in a restaurant chain is the easiest way to be exposed to the wonders of manipulation. Most of the chains that have a location in every city near you have a microwave in their kitchen and it is the most used appliance.

One example that really shocked me was working at a Boston Market, a fast-food restaurant with locations around the country. It is the same concept as Kentucky Fried Chicken, but makes it seem like it's classier. Something like the relationship between Wal-Mart and Target, for example. Boston Market's claim to fame is its rotisserie chicken, which is actually slow-roasted. This feature alone set it apart from a KFC, I suppose.

However, all of the side dishes from macaroni and cheese to mashed potatoes were prepared in a microwave. Don't be thinking for one second that this is a unique practice. The microwave is one of the main features of the kitchen in Chili's and most other chains across the country. There is absolutely no other way to serve that many people nationwide at the same time.

I was a big fan of macaroni and cheese for a long time- I was raised with those blue-box-blues. I would never eat the stuff from the microwave and most people are with me on that. Don't even bring up that Easy Mac garbage. Kraft was probably horrified when they discovered the population was tired of waiting eight minutes for mac and cheese. Put it in plastic, make it microwaveable and cut the time in half.

The amount of orders for mac and cheese would decrease dramatically if the menu said it was microwaved. Not because they're worried about brain cancer from the machine, but because it's gross. More importantly, it takes less than ten minutes to cook pasta regularly. That's out of the question at many restaurants- these orders need to be on the table in six minutes, or we're not up to standard.

Six minutes is way too short an amount of time to produce anything of value. Imagine if we strove to satisfy all urges in six minutes. Think of all of those disappointed women.

Chain restaurants do make it easy for working though. The notion that each cook is expendable and can be replaced without wrenching the system is terrifying for employees, ideal for employers. To perfect a system for efficiency is something to be revered, like an assembly line that zigs and zags psychotically but still churns out the orders and produces results.

For example, on my first day working for Sodexo- a company which supplies cooks to business places, schools, universities, and hospitals around the country- I was handed a piece of paper that detailed every single minute of my day. Here's a little sample of what I can remember; it was front and back, fully detailing all four-hundred and eighty minutes of my workday, to be repeated five times per week.

9:00- 9:02 Clock in, follow proper handwashing procedures

9:02-9:07 – Pre-cook bacon.

9:07-9:11- Prepare onions, peppers, and tomatoes for omelets.

9:11-9:14- Move cold ingredients from refrigerator to serving line.

This meticulous schedule was extreme, but they have perfected a system. This is the manner in which places like Applebee's or McDonalds are capable of repeating the same dishes at fast speeds in thousands of locations at the same time. If there is a standard that must be applied to every aspect of the workday, it leaves little room for individual questions or interference. It requires hardly any explanation. To cook an egg at a chain restaurant, push EGG on the microwave. For a burger, push BURGER. The margin for error is diminished. The perfect job for a stoned teenager.

No matter which kitchen it is, the opening shift is usually best. The morning is the perfect time of the day in a restaurant, uninterrupted and free. I have one hour every morning to use the entire kitchen as my own and get things done. It's also the only time of day when the place is as close to clean as it can possibly get.

Outside of the tremendous white noise of the equipment, the place is unusually peaceful. Things can get done without being micromanaged or asked three times if it's ready, three minutes after the order is placed. "On the fly" doesn't mean it's immediately going to fly out of my ass. It's quite an enjoyable job.

The Journalist

""News is something somebody doesn't want printed; all else is advertising."

I've never really been able to make sense of my decision to become a journalist. Relatives laughed and pointed out that I wouldn't make any money. That didn't really concern me, all of them were broke anyways, so I didn't see what was so funny.

I suppose it began with some hopeless idealism, some sort of notion that the world could be changed if everybody were just made aware of the truth. A simplistic generalization of millions of individuals, most of which could care less about the truth. I thought I would be hunting down leads like that guy in Citizen Kane, chasing a story based on one word that no one could have possibly heard. It's still a great film.

I remember reading *The Jungle*, and my teacher telling me that Upton Sinclair was a "muck-raker". I struggled to understand why he wasn't just called a journalist. If we're not *raking muck*, then we may as well just hand the reigns over to TMZ.

I dreamt of driving cross-country to cover a motocross race while experiencing the American dream. I even tried to live with a motorcycle club that hangs out at the edge of the city, because that's what my idols had done. I idolized Nellie Bly, and her crazy and dangerous journalism that produced change because she exposed a hidden atrocity. I imagined myself pulling back the curtains of wizards everywhere, whether or not I had a Tin-Man and a Lion by my side.

The truth used to hide; it required some digging. There were secrets. I idolized figures which generally represented dissent from the given order, throughout time facing countless authorities in the name of the people. I thrived on the words of Walter Lippman and Hunter Thompson, studied Bernstein and Woodward as prophets, and hung my hat on a single fundamental idea: the truth can inspire change. It turns out the truth is subjective, and more importantly, it just does not matter. The most mind-boggling and unbelievable news has become commonplace and we're quite desensitized to the constant flow of negative information.

It was about halfway through my studies when I came to realize that with technological advances, came psychological sacrifices. The overwhelming tidal wave of information which consumes us daily, ripping us from the shore, dragging out, and returning to shore. Enough air for that final breath, just to open for another overload.

I was studying a dying art, and as if to prove my developing theory, the university officially killed its journalism program in my third year of studies. They didn't end the program, but they certainly gave it a demotion, labeling it a "Social Science."

Since its inception, the journalism degree had been a member of the College of Humanities and Fine Arts Program. A proper journalist is an artist, the scribe of the people, of the utmost importance in a democracy. It is also strongly related to humanity, especially when it has become so dependent on this information. We rely on these sources to tell us all sorts of information, from society to entertainment to government goings-on.

Many countries around the world refer to the media as the fourth estate, that is, it holds enough power to be socially recognized as an informal part of the government, a necessity for a nation to know of their government's behaviors. Even before there were written newspapers and television programs to deliver news, some poor schlub stood in the town square and shouted the news because it was necessary. Otherwise, I am quite sure that someone would have just told them to shut their damned mouth.

Somehow, maybe through the media itself, journalists have been portrayed as these types of warriors I speak of, Robert Redford or Russell Crowe digging for stories. Peter Finch losing his mind live on television in *Network*.

Adversely, the profession is demonized, certainly related to the element of attack journalism that hides in the shadow of importance- providing information that was forced by the journalist, rather than observed through patient research. It's eye-catching, and it sells media.

At my first job with the local TV news station, I accompanied a crew to interview a man who had unexpectedly resigned from local government. I was in charge of holding a boom mic, the big fuzzy microphones on sticks that are held above the scene to capture audio. We drove right up to the man's house, which surprised me, but that surprise quickly became horror as the two men in the front seat turned to me, said, "Ready?" and approached the house.

"Get up by the side of the front door," he told me as he began to pound on the glass, "Stay to the side." He continued pounding on the storm door, ringing the bell, and calling the man's name, as his partner ran to the living room window and began to knock with two quarters between his fingers, producing a loud clang.

A man popped his head between the two front doors and peaked outside.

"No comment, please leave my property. I have asked nicely. I don't want any trouble."

He had gone back inside, but the crew continued to slam on the door, in addition to slamming on the living room windows where he was sitting. They followed him around the house knocking on each window.

"You have nothing to say about the funds missing from the town's budget? Is this your signature here at the bottom of a phony receipt made to an unknown business? What will your wife and children say, knowing that you stole from the town?"

This calm and unthreatening man became agitated, as the reporter had hoped, "Do not talk about my family. Get the fuck off of my property right now you mother…"

He tried to step out of the house, pushing the door with just enough force to collide with the cameraman. The camera shifted and five seconds of chaos occurred. The cameraman barely moved.

"Got it, that's all we needed. Assault. Let's get the fuck out of here. Good luck, asshole. Hope you saved some of that money."

We ran back to the car, the entire ordeal lasting less than five minutes. It had taken longer to drive there than it did to capture the "story", and that night there were about fifteen seconds of that film played on the news.

"Tonight, at seven, a local council member resigns in disgrace over embezzled funds…" while a team approaches the house and knocks once nicely like a neighbor looking for some sugar. A man pushes open the door, causes the camera to shoot around chaotically, and the man says, "Get the $%&! off my property!"

The power of editing is stupendous. This man is certainly disgraceful, assuming he stole the money, but I think he'll have a hard time even going to the grocery store now. I don't think our attack really helped progress the story or expose any detail that wasn't already available. It sure was entertaining, though.

I learned something very important that day, and it was not about the wonders of editing.

It was the fact that this man was destroyed before any research had been done, for the sake of entertainment. The lead reporter on the story could have cared less about informing the public. He had heard about the resignation from a friend in city hall, acted immediately, and it was on the news that very night, portrayed as factual.

Three months later, after some investigation, it had turned out that this man was nothing more than a pawn. He quit out of fear, that he had made some mistake that cost the town money. His signature was on a document that he was asked to sign regularly, and he rarely read it. It always had the same details, and there weren't many discrepancies.

Sign the paper, pass it on. They've even given it a name, *robo-signing.* If there were another signature on that paper, the news crew and I would have attacked their house in the same way. I realized that if I were going to partake in journalism, it would be in the dwindling world of print. Television news is nothing more than a gimmick for your entertainment.

This investigation should have taken place before the man was made to be a villain, and long before any reporter stormed his castle and demanded he answer, publicly, for his alleged crimes. Interfering with the very simple notion of "innocent until proven guilty" is exactly why some people hate journalists.

This type of journalism resembles paparazzi, following celebrities for stories and making them, if they can't be found. We need some entertainment- we can't be talking about serious issues all of the time; the world would become gray- worse off than it is now. Imagine if that depressing news report you consume with dinner was missing that token dog on a skateboard or cute little science fair winner who's going to save the world one day.

Every story has a purpose, and each of them were selected. If you do hear the same story on these networks, they are presented in a different tone, with a different opinion on the matter.

Objectivity cannot exist. Each publication gets to choose their subject matter. If it isn't important enough to someone on the staff, it's not going to be in the paper. Then, we get to choose how to frame the story. If there's a shooting, is the paper going to focus on the 2nd amendment, the shooter's history, or the stories of the victims? Sure, we can write in third person and jam each paragraph with numbers, but they must be arranged in a way that makes you feel the same way I do. The journalist needs to have an opinion on the matter, otherwise the content is useless. Lastly, but perhaps equally as important, the reader's opinion forms the paper's content through their desire to be reassured. People typically get their news from one source, the one which agrees with them most.

Journalism as a watchdog to the government and whistleblower to corporations it has never been a matter of debate amongst leaders. It is necessary in a democratic environment. Those historical champions of American democracy which we quote constantly and print on dollar bills certainly believed in journalism's necessity. It was the very first Amendment made to their holiest of documents.

The Declaration had flaws and many of these individuals have some history that isn't worth discussing. They were from a different time. For a modern person with a basic education, to criticize any of these men is presumptuous and inherently ignorant. They certainly had flaws, we can all admit to that, but to ignore their accomplishments is fallacious.

These men escaped a tyrannical empire and built a new country. I don't think the modern mind can even begin to appreciate this notion. It seemed to work well enough, we're still living in its shadow. Their documents informed the values of millions of people, living according to these agreeable principles. Hundreds of years later, people quote it as much as their given bibles. For some reason, that country they built is one of the "world leaders" dominating the world with cultural and military export. *What have you done lately?*

Napoleon Bonaparte famously said, *"Three hostile newspapers are more to be feared than one thousand bayonets."* I think the Little Corporal would have fallen in love with the modern media phenomenon, thrived on it, and we would all be *parlez-vous-ing Français.* Journalism can be a wonderful way to change the world- just by telling people something they didn't know.

The university didn't find it so important. It was also around this time that I had tried to apply to the school newspaper. Somewhere in my first conversation with a writer there, it was made clear to me that the university owned the paper and there would be no "hard-hitting" journalism. I didn't even understand the prolific problem this presents, until after a semester of journalism classes. I was well aware that this relationship was messed up. There isn't any other way to slice and serve that nonsense.

Mr. Trebek, I'll take Conflict of Interest for $500.

The realization had been a thrashing ocean of thought within my mind, and the tide swelled as I was further exposed to journalism's ideals, which I have seen fall dead on the shore before me. The ability to access all information available to humankind has caused nothing but confusion.

To believe that everyone has an opinion is an entirely toxic idea. If someone is not educated on a subject, their opinion can hardly be worth anything. There *are* stupid questions, and there are even more stupid answers. Don't let anyone tell you otherwise.

If you would like a good example of the difference between journalism and blog work, compare Watergate and Wikileaks. Both involved the exposure of government documents, in very different ways. Watergate was thoroughly researched by several newspapers, prodding to find the hidden truth. It took two years of extremely hard work, but ultimately President Nixon was forced to resign before being impeached.

Wikileaks did not involve any journalists, no research seemed to be involved, but the public was given tremendous amounts of government documents. They may as well have been in a foreign language. Nothing resulted from Wikileaks. If not for Watergate, we may have ended up living in Alan Moore's world with Nixon still in office. *Who's watching the Watchmen?*

We're living in a time where almost no one reads books, yet everyone seems to have one published. It's ideal to live without the censorship of large organizations, of course, but this can lead to misinformation and nonsense flooding the market. To put it simply, if you take something good and mass-produce it, it faces almost no chance of maintaining its quality or purpose.

The loss of journalism's aura began with the industrialization of the news. The funneling of information to only a few companies, while they purchased the smaller ones and consumed them. From there, we can see the beginning of the end with television news- the development of entertainment rather than information.

The Sunday funnies became intertwined with a *newscaster telling us that today we had fifteen homicides and sixty-three violent crimes, as if that's the way it's supposed to be!*

There were some novel attempts at making television journalism a force worth recognizing. Its early days of Edward Murrow or Walter Cronkite were sold to lackluster wanna-bes like Ted Turner's army and the middle-aged ladies on Morning Shows that have never investigated anything. Instead of actually allowing women to have authoritative voices on air, they gave them the role of interviewing pop stars.

CNN ruined journalism forever. It would have happened later, with the arrival of the internet, but it did not need to happen in 1980. The new-found success in twenty-four-hour news led to NBC and FOX developing continuous news stations as well. The worst possible thing to occur in the world of information.

There is no need to "be informed" at all hours of the day, *especially* if everything is negative. We won't even address how many times they repeat themselves.

Casting research to the wind for the sake of remaining in print or on the air. The competitive nature is fundamentally gone, and most places are handed their news by a large outlet like Reuters or Associated Press. They fight to keep the reader interested and entertained, while supplying the same story as every other outlet. Nothing else happened today? Really, we're all going to just quote the president and call the job done?

The rush for information and resulting *front-page syndrome,* along with the need to have it immediately has only had one effect: misinformation. I think they're calling it "fake news" on the hill, but they're out of touch anyhow. Fact-checking is a silly new game often played with topics that are nothing more than conjecture. It's not very hard to see where a story originated.

There are five simple questions to ask about any story. Who said it? Can I trust the source? Is that person biased on this subject?

Am I biased on this subject? Where can I get reliable information to help me frame my opinion?

For a blogger, there aren't editors checking sources, I hardly ever see them provided. The writers have no real attachment to the story and therefore, you are just being sold what they have first. Breaking news is hardly worth the immediacy and could very well wait to be in the morning broadcast. Most of the time it should wait, because there are always layers to a news story.

I won't take the time to address the multitude of effects that all of this has had on our ability to understand the world around us. There is enough regular information to keep a person occupied at all hours of the day, without the intentionally created stories of advertising and public relations. Don't forget: a successful public relations campaign is a failure for you. Somebody did something wrong, and you complained. They successfully pandered to you enough to make you shut your mouth. Now, they can carry on.

Consider yourself crystallized, tenderized by a *Silver Anvil*.

Turn off the news. Go outside with your family. There is no need to be informed all of the time, and do not let anyone try to convince you that this is a matter of opinion.

The editor finished reading the article. It was meant to discuss the state of journalism and its importance. He expected some moral explanation that quoted the founding fathers. They were in there somewhere.

The paper was on the verge of a buyout, and the owner was likely to shut down operations rather than sell his company that he had built from the ground.

"I can't print this, man, you're telling people to stop paying attention to news. Are you trying to eliminate our jobs faster? More importantly, this is the most depressing thing I have ever read. It's just a pissed off rant. Where's your sense of hope?"

He looked up with despair in his eyes, an immense concern for his employee that used to run the daily meetings with enthusiasm. Now, that same journalist rarely appeared at the office and composed stories decrying the entire journalism industry.

I tried to contain my anger and avoid saying something temperamental that will only cause more problems. I grabbed yesterday's paper from his desk, ruffle it around, and slam it back down with enthusiasm. Theatrics can really help to get a point across.

"My sense of HOPE? This is the paper from yesterday:

"Is School Making Our Children Ill?

Hostage Crisis in Nigeria Intensifies

Local Congressman Pleads Guilty to Embezzlement

Voter Fraud a Concern for Local Election

People in China are Buying Fresh Cans of Air from Canada

Human Activity has wiped out two-thirds of world's wildlife since 1980

That is only our little local paper, and that is only some of the headlines.

Yesterday, in less than one hour- I learned that 30% of the Congo has been logged for pharmaceuticals and meat production; the United States produces so much trash that we have to export it; you can't really recycle plastic; most of the Amazon has been felled to raise cows, and it's on fire again, which I think means there are officially more Amazon warehouses than trees in the rainforest; and supposedly, eating chocolate daily will help me lose weight. This was all learned yesterday, and I wasn't searching. Just casually reading through headlines, as I do every single day.

If you don't run my story, as it is, on the front page, I am done. The industry is dying, we may as well go out fighting. Make people aware of what they will lose. Maybe my stupid rant will go viral and we'll sell the papers we print for no one each day.

You can label it opinion, but it better be on the front. There is no excuse, we are talking about one article on one day. I have written 'award-winning' articles about crap that meant nothing, just for you."

I walked out; we will see what happens. I think I made myself clear, and I didn't want to allow him any further opportunities to try and talk me down. Quite frankly, the job feels like a façade and I'm so mentally burnt that I forgot how to spell façade this morning. I reassured myself it wasn't even an English word, but that made it no less depressing.

I haven't covered a story of importance in months, and those regional journalism awards mean nothing. Nothing came of the shocking stories being exposed.

My mind is shot to shit.

Silent Spring

If you're over fifty years old, you can remember April 22, 1970; the day which one of the largest protests in human history took place. Over twenty million people took to the streets of the United States, screaming on behalf of the Earth.

I like to think that Dr. Seuss enjoyed the spectacle of 20,000,000 lifted-Loraxes speaking for the trees. Demanding their governments intervene on behalf of their children. The politicians have always taken the wrong side, favoring industry over individual.

If you're even older, you may remember a chemical called DDT from your childhood. They claimed it prevented polio, which it most certainly did not. The rest of us have probably seen it on mosquito spray that says "No DDT" on the can.

The lethal pesticide was invented in the 40s, and the man who suggested spraying it everywhere was a given a Nobel Prize for his contributions to humankind. The government declared it a wondrous chemical and highly recommended it.

Dichlorodiphenyltrichloroethane, or DDT, is a pesticide that was advocated by the U.S. government for agricultural and domestic use. They based their suggestion on science handed to them by DDT producers. There are fucked up videos available on YouTube that show government officials spraying DDT clouds directly at children to exemplify just how safe it was. Parents would encourage their children to run behind spraying trucks, enveloping themselves in a chemical fog.

Throughout the 40s and 50s, the hazardous chemical was in the air of every town across America. Domestic sales were steady and it was being used on practically all agriculture. No one suspected that it was actually harming them, especially because the government was pushing it.

In 1962, a marine biologist named Rachel Carson published *Silent Spring*, discussing the many harmful effects of DDT. More importantly, she revealed that the "science" which told the government DDT was great, happened to be entirely fabricated by the companies that produced the toxin. The companies actually hired "scientists" to provide false information to the government about the products safety. The United States government printed it in pamphlets and distributed nationwide. *For our profit, at your expense.*

I have affectionately titled my book in honor of Ms. Carson's work. She was a paid scientist; I am just really disappointed. It's quite alright to be unaware, but it is not okay to ignore the cries after being informed. These are the cries of your children and their unborn children. If we make some simple adjustments now, we can feel proud to leave this world to them, rather than ashamed and providing weak explanations as to why things are this way. Maybe I'm wasting my time. …*That's just the way it is, somethings will never change…*

I can sympathize that we haven't known the names of our domestic enemies until now. DowDupont is out there. They invented styrofoam, explosive breast implants, and the non-recyclable plastic which composes milk jugs. They also produced napalm and Agent Orange used in Vietnam, which still causes birth deformities fifty years later. Oh, and they **invented** that DDT stuff, then convinced the government to spray it on everyone.

Most regular people are entirely unaware of DowDupont, one of the largest producers of plastic on Earth, headquartered in

Midland, Michigan. It's rather strange that everybody seems to protest Monsanto, but DowDupont make them look like amateurs. They are responsible for the most contaminated sites in America, over eighty of them. They've turned the rivers and bays of Michigan into a toxic soup, worthy of a top spot on the Superfund list; even forced a few towns to be permanently evacuated. The land they have contaminated is the Saginaw Bay, on the shores of the Great Lakes. They probably won't be so Great much longer.

DowDupont is worth $49,000,000,000 annually. Forty-nine billion dollars every single year, and they're destroying the largest freshwater lakes in North America. Slowly, but surely.

Unless you are a NASCAR fan cheering for Jeff Gordon, you've probably never heard of DowDupont. They were one of the foremost producers of that wonderful DDT that is now banned in 90% of the world. Their lethal brew is actually responsible for many of the Superfund sites. The same company are now leaders of the oil and plastic industry. Are we seeing a pattern from these evil bastards, or what? They're repeat offenders that have completely forgotten what life is like in the real world, so they just keep committing crimes. No one disciplines them.

You can imagine DowDupont like Hexxus from *Ferngully: The Last Rainforest*. Speaking of which, can the executives at 20th Century Fox please begin production of the *Ferngully* "live-action" remake, starring Emma Watson as Crysta? A new generation needs its message.

If you're too young for the *Ferngully* reference, no worries. You've probably seen the remake called *Avatar*. DowDupont is that awful, cigar-smoking general with the Mech Warrior suit. While you sleep at night, they're slowly and methodically bombing the Tree of Souls, and it won't be long until they're shouting timber.

These companies, like Monsanto and DowDupont which produced DDT attempted to demoralize and demean Rachel Carson in order to negate her impenetrable argument. They have done the same thing with plastic, using advertising to sway opinion. They are doing it right now. History repeats itself when no one pays attention.

Not long after *Silent Spring* was published, President Kennedy ordered government scientists to investigate her claims. They realized she was 100% correct and acted rather swiftly in response. Well, as swift as the government *can* act, about ten years. By the year 1972, DDT was banned in the United States. Gone, no more. You're literally killing us. The stuff was bad.

For the sake of understanding the severity of our new problem, I will be clear: the amount of damage caused by the food and plastic industries in the United States today makes me want to shower in DDT, like the kids used to.

The only way to test if something is immortal is by trying to kill it. Too big to fail is just a pessimistic way to describe a problem requiring a creative solution. The bigger they are, the harder they fall. These are gigantic corporations actively working to destroy the planet for profit. It's not an exaggeration or dramatization, there was never a time that the danger of plastic was unknown. Not one single moment.

The following quote is from 1959, at the centennial celebration of the oil industry, organized by the American Petroleum Institute. For an added dose of irony, the man who delivered this speech was Edward Teller, the father of the hydrogen bomb:

Carbon dioxide has a strange property. It transmits visible light but it absorbs the infrared radiation which is emitted from the earth. Its presence in the atmosphere causes a greenhouse effect [....] It has been calculated that a temperature rise corresponding to a ten percent increase in carbon dioxide will be sufficient to melt the icecap and submerge New York. All the coastal cities would be covered, and since a considerable percentage of the human race lives in coastal regions, I think that this chemical contamination is more serious than most people tend to believe.

Plastic is made of oil. This must not be discussed in any science classes, anywhere, because there seems to be a steady progression toward electric cars and other renewable energies. Not many discussions highlighting the fact that the same oil we're objecting to driving with is the chemical which composes our babies' bottles.

Another one of the largest producers of plastic for American use is ExxonMobil. Their environmental record is so bad that there is an actual Wikipedia page titled "ExxonMobil climate change controversy" because they have adamantly argued against scientists discussing climate change. They don't want to see pictures from Hurricane Sandy, when seven feet of floodwater poured into the 9/11 museum; or hear about those streets in Miami that look like Venice, Italy.

ExxonMobil is part of what's leftover of Standard Oil Company. The company that helped invent modern plastic, discovering fracking and how to isolate hydrocarbons. Founded by that Rockefeller guy- the richest man *ever*, because he dug up some oil from the ground. His net worth today would be three times the amount of Amazon founder Jeff Bezos, currently the richest man in the world, worth $120 billion.

ExxonMobil destroyed Venezuela. Gutted the land, soiled the water supply, killed off wildlife. The Venezuelans had enough, so they kicked them out to sell their oil themselves. Then, the corporate whores tried to sue the country for billions.

There is enough for another book, the oil giant's genocide had its own dedicated chapter in my college geography textbook. The story of Venezuela doesn't seem to hit home hard enough, though. Let's talk domestic. Is Alaska close enough to home?

If you asked an average American over thirty to name two famous ships, they would likely begin with the *Titanic*, of course. Then, after a second to think of *any* other ship they know, they may remember that barge forever burned in their memories. *The Exxon Valdez*.

To the English-speaking ear, it almost sounds intriguingly exotic, like a Carnival Cruise. Oh, by the way, have you heard of Carnival Cruises? They are known for dumping their trash and liquid waste directly in the ocean. They pay a fine and do it again and again. Unfortunately, this was no Carnival ship. For those who remember, the *Exxon Valdez* incident was the worst oil spill in history, when it took place in 1989. The corporate giant dropped eleven million gallons of oil onto a reef in Alaska.

Did they do it on purpose? One can only speculate. I don't like to spread rumors.

They didn't do much to make up for it, in fact, they didn't even clean up after themselves. 11,000 Alaskan volunteers donated their own time to remedy ExxonMobil's disaster. To avoid any more criticism, they changed the name of their shipping company to something redundant and vague: *SeaRiver Maritime*. You would never guess that horribly-named entity was just ExxonMobil, the same fuckers that enjoy feeding petroleum to animals in searivers around the globe.

British Petroleum, more leftovers of Standard Oil Company, shattered ExxonMobil's oil dumping record in 2010, pouring 210,000,000 gallons of oil into the Gulf of Mexico. There was a rumor that this was an attack orchestrated by the Queen of England on the people of North America, an attempt to diminish the seafood supply. It's probably just internet conjecture, but we'll never really know.

The jolly petrol guvnors at BP released some feigned apology commercials featuring the CEO rubbing his nipples and went back to business as normal. In 2015, it was revealed that they had actually managed to make the situation worse. The cleaning chemical, Corexit, increased the oil's toxicity and killed more fish and wildlife.

The Titanic actually has something in common with an oil spill, aside from all of the deaths. In 1851, long before Jack and Rose, the *Limitation of Liability Act* was passed. It hasn't been used many times in history, but there are two very notable cases- the sinking of the Titanic, and the British Petroleum oil spill. This allows the owners to be forgiven for murder because they were just trying to do their job.

Somehow, while causing worldwide destruction and producing a very large portion of the plastics in the world; these companies that exist in the shadows. Maybe everyone does know, we just don't see any other way to get to work tomorrow. It's like a Tinder date or a drunken dive-bar hook-up. *What was their name again? It's too late to ask now, I'll just figure it out when they stop fucking me.* It's romantic, really.

For their profit, at your expense.

That actually has a nice ring to it. Imagine that handsome guy from *Mad Men* in a dapper three-piece suit, standing before some majestic mountains while Vivaldi plays in the background. *For our profit, at your expense.* Sounds great, sign me up.

After the Earth Day protests in 1970, recycling began and the EPA was founded, but this reinforced the plastics industry. It took one year for the newborn plastic bottle market to grow exponentially, thanks to one of the most scandalous advertising schemes of all time. As if overnight, people seemed to develop dependence on a product that hadn't existed in the history of humanity.

Perrier, which is now owned by Nestle, deemed itself a fancy and luxurious water that improved health and loads of other things. Like a modern Napoleon, some little French punk invaded the minds of Americans and confused the living hell out of them. Those French must be smart people, because we didn't even know that we needed this wonder elixir.

Jeremiah Peabody's Polyunsaturated Quick-Dissolving Fast-Acting Pleasant-Tasting Green and Purple Pills were quickly forced out of business by this new hydration revelation. Perrier can cure cancer and keep an old man stiff in the bedroom for hours. Ladies, it's good for you, too. Unwanted pregnancy? Forget Planned Parenthood, buy some Perrier. Just pour it on your elbows and sing *Frère Jacques*. No more baby. *Voila, you American pig. Oui, oui; oink, oink. Give us all your dough for l'eau.*

The U.S. market devoured plastic water with their wallets. Ridiculous advertising that deemed this water healthier than regular water had created a market that did not exist. They created an unnecessary product that directly defied the wishes of twenty million Earth Day protesters. It only took a few years for shelves to be filled with "luxury water" and stores had no problem selling the product.

At least Perrier was selling us water from France, it seemed fancy. Nestle took over and figured they would just steal it from the American population. While we're on the topic of Nestle, just to throw it out there; the following are all names under which Nestle distributes water across America: Acqua Panna, Arrowhead, Deer Park, Ice Mountain, Nestle Pure Life, Ozarka, Perrier, Poland Spring.

Nestle have *cornered* the market, which basically means they have dominated *almost* to monopolization. To such a point that they have near complete control and the market fluctuates according to that lone company's wishes. Backed the competition into a corner. Well, Pepsi and Coca-Cola are doing fine. With the help of Nestle, they have backed the American people into a corner, and they're spreading worldwide. Business in Africa is booming. There are several countries where Dasani is the only water available. *Ka-Ching.*

What Happened?

Speaking of cornering markets, the creator of the first modern grocery store in the United States, Clarence Saunders of Piggly Wiggly, was ousted by laws regarding the cornering of markets. They killed his business, but in retrospect; who cares about that guy? He ushered in the grocery excesses of the modern American home, where most of our food is wasted.

Stock brokers tried to sabotage him, and he fought back with too much confidence. Pointed for the fence like Babe and struck out swinging. It is impressive, though- one man had completely changed the American grocery shopping experience. In 1932, Piggly Wiggly's profits soared to roughly $180 million per year. The equivalent of about $3 billion today. This was no surprise, given that Saunders had conceived the idea for shopping carts and conveyor belt register lines, amongst a few other things we take for granted. He invented the idea of doing your own shopping.

Can you imagine approaching a grocery counter, handing over a list, and waiting while the clerk grabs all of it from the back? For the life of me, I can't picture it. That concept sounds ridiculous to the modern person. It would certainly help with planning meals and decreasing my grocery store bill, but I don't have that kind of patience.

That's how it was before Piggly Wiggly, so obviously, the people welcomed the luxuries with wide open wallets. By the time the 50s rolled around, Piggly Wiggly's concepts were commonplace in all grocery stores. Abundance and impulse purchases became a regular part of the shopping experience due to this newfound freedom to peruse the store.

We cannot entirely blame the generation that lived in this time for their excesses. Many of them suffered through a Depression and the Second World War. To be able to live comfortably and enjoy some luxuries after the war ended was necessary. They wanted to forget and rebuild.

They were also some of the best recyclers that ever lived. During World War Two, people were asked to contribute all sorts of metals, rags, rubbers, and other things to produce what was necessary for the war. America sorted through trash to gather materials. It was considered one of the most patriotic things to do to help the war from home. There were propaganda posters, which should be reissued tomorrow:

World War Two was the last time in history that every American was so unified they forgot their problems and got their hands dirty for a single cause. Unfortunately, their comfortable new lifestyles set a terrible example for their children. Processed food swarmed the market, in order to fill these new Piggly Wiggly grocery stores. There would be no way to fill these structures without the bulk of it being boxed or frozen.

When it came time, those 60s kids weren't having that *Leave It to Beaver,* happy-go-lucky American lifestyle. Many of them disdained their parents lack of respect for the environment and most of their rules in general.

Protests to their parent's entrenched ways were regular occurrences through the decade. Even a child born in the year 2000 has heard of *Woodstock.* The art of the decade clearly exemplifies a desire to be better human beings, but I'm told they were all just high on drugs.

Maybe they were just too extreme. They said things like, "If you don't recycle and fix the world now, you may need a gas mask and flashlight to get to the office." Well, that still hasn't happened so they must have just been dramatic, right?

The *Summer of Love* scared the shit out of the general population, and the hippies were battling all aspects of American life at the same time. Don't have kids, stop driving cars, ban plastic bags, stop the war; *tax the rich, feed the poor 'til there are no rich no more.*

It was a lot to ask. *Ten Years After* asked for most of that in less than four minutes. The old folks saw this is as death. They already had everything taken away from them, *you freaks and hairies want to do it again?* It was a little overwhelming, a bunch of teenagers tripping balls and singing songs that open with, *"There's nothing you can do that can't be done"*

Turn this music off. What kind of nonsense is that? *All you need is love?* I need food and water and television and I need my job and my family and my car. Doesn't matter if they were high or not because the hippies ultimately quit. As far as I can tell, they weren't high enough.

The 1970s seem like a confusing time. The burnout from that previous decade's high had caused a serious comedown. All that sign-waving and love-making produced no results, the zeitgeist's idols were dying off as the decade turned.

The hippies abandoned the ideals of love, got pregnant, and submitted to the proverbial Man. When Jimi Hendrix suggested he wouldn't care if they cut off their hair, he hardly thought they would actually do it. Did anybody involved really expect the 60s to lead to *this?*

The 20 million people who attended Earth Day protests in 1970 are drinking bottled water right now.

Sixty years after Rachel Carson blew the whistle on DDT; the world is more confused than it has ever been. Fifty years after that inaugural Earth Day, the world now spends at least $35 billion on bottled water annually. $16 billion alone is in the United States. Just so we're clear, that's almost 50% of the entire bottled water market, and the United States is only 4% of the global population. There are 320,000,000 people here, on average consuming and producing 10x more plastic trash than there are people.

Maybe that's a bit too much math, but it's as simple as this: the American population is being manipulated into spending its own money to buy its own water. This water is being contained in nonrecyclable plastic, which we will have to clean up in the future. We're willingly being embarrassed by Willy Wonka.

In a country that considers itself more developed than most others, it's amazing that we don't appreciate the simple things like running water. Nearly all of the U.S. population has access to clean, quality water. There is absolutely nothing wrong with the water in the tap. When it comes to bottled water; nearly all of it is tap water, but you can ask Nestle, Pepsi, and Coke about that. They're the ones selling you municipal water supplies from places like Michigan and Maine. They definitely don't try to keep it a secret, but nobody seems to be aware, except for the hundreds of thousands of people in North America that regularly attend Nestle protests and court hearings, trying to have them removed from their town. Fighting for the water that flows beneath their own homes.

Supposedly we live in the "first-world" and celebrate democracy, but there are South American countries in democratic infancy that protect their citizens better than the United States government. Uruguay's government responded to the people's cries and banned the privatization of water. They also run entirely on renewable energy. Just saying…

They managed to defeat one of the biggest corporations in the world, Vivendi, which owns most of the world's water. Never heard of Vivendi? Their reach is beyond your wildest dreams. They own the companies that are too big to fail. They make money off of almost every single product that is bought or sold anywhere. If the entire world were on fire right now, the world governments would have to ask Vivendi for the water to put it out.

Vivendi have been running the world so long, it was founded by Napoleon's nephew, and they supplied water to Istanbul when it was still called Constantinople. They're currently setting their eyes on owning North America, so far, they have acquired control of the water supply in twenty-three American cities.

Oh, and most of the water-peddling corporations like Pepsi receive billions of dollars in U.S. government subsidies through the SNAP food stamp program, gathered from tax money. Then they gather the water from our water supplies and sell it back to us.

In case we've forgotten, the recent example of water supply atrocities occurred in a town called Flint, Michigan. Thanks to Nestle, you might be enjoying their luxury water right now, bottled by the corporation specially for you. You'll never know, you are not supposed to know. The illusion of safety in a plastic bottle is enough to suppress those questions. One thing you can know is- that safe feeling is a façade. It might actually be harmful; we haven't even had the time to understand what plastic does to food or water yet. It's probably not good.

It's great that we are all aware of that Flint situation. The national attention forces some action, at least. The situation is not resolved yet, but those responsible were forced to respond. Flint was victim to lead poisoning in their water because of poor construction. It was laziness, it wasn't some malicious act carried out by the fuckers who make Crunch Bars.

During my time living in California, water fountains and restrooms were closed and being removed from public beaches to conserve water. Businesses with grass in front make sure to post a sign that says, "Using reclaimed water to support conservation. Do not drink."

We should talk about the U.S. Forest Service, which has contracts with Nestle in California, allowing them to sell water from a national park. If you drink Arrowhead water, you're directly responsible for the destruction of the San Bernardino National Forest.

Supposedly the entire west coast is running out of water while Nestle is pumping it into plastic bottles and selling nationwide. Their destruction is across America as well, in places like Evart, Michigan; Fryeburg, Maine; McCloud, California.

Fryeburg has been sued five times by Nestle for "interfering with their right to grow their market share." They just want Nestle to stop stealing their water, before they run out. Their creeks are running dry. The corporation is worth $100 billion. Think about that for a moment. They made 99% of that money pumping municipal water supplies into plastic bottles.

In 2016, despite the entire town protesting, Nestle was granted access to Fryeburg's water for the next 45 years, but it will probably run dry in twenty. Many creeks there have already run dry. According to sources, Nestle paid Paul Lepage, Governor of Maine at the time, a few million dollars to approve the deal. He must have a sweet house on the water in Kennebunkport. He's not even in office anymore, and he will be dead long before Nestle's new contract expires.

While reading about Nestle's genocide taking place across America, I stumbled across this gem from Nestle spokesman Brian Flaherty., *"We're one of 70,000 different types of beverages you can buy. ... We use the least amount of water and the least amount of plastic, and we're good for you."*

It sounds like something from a sketch on *Chappelle's Show,* but yes, he is right. There are seventy-thousand other types of beverages you can buy. Let's talk about some of those awful demons.

Doesn't Aquafina sound like freakin' magic? Actually, it sounds like it could be the first homosexual aquatic superhero, but I digress. Can't wait 'til they team up with the *Avengers.*

It needs a name like Aquafina because it is tap water. Nestle calls their stuff *Pure Life* because it is "purified" tap water. More like, pure bullshit. They are laughing at the population of the world, every time we take a sip. It seems people won't drink their own tap water, or just buy a filter to alleviate any concerns they have, but they'll drink it out of a bottle with a sweet name like Dasani. The bigwigs of Nestle probably don't even drink the water they steal.

They use words to describe their "purification process" like *reverse osmosis* and *ozone sterilization*, which I've tried to research, I still have no idea what the fuck that could possibly mean. *You're talking a lot, but you're not saying anything.* It is safe to assume that it means absolutely nothing. They're fancy names for the process of bottling tap water.

They sell it off without remorse. It's like an infomercial at four in the morning for something you just can't believe they've produced. The proverbial gun went off, and massive corporations began a nationwide treasure hunt to find available water they could steal from communities. It must have been like a modern wild west, featuring real cowboys of the plastic industry.

Just like Native Americans battling for land, cities across America took up arms against the corporations. When Wisconsin rejected Nestle, they went next door to Michigan and offered them baseball fields and parks. Apparently, the town was unaware that sports fields and parks only require one thing: water. Quite the bogus deal if you ask me.

These companies could have never survived selling DDT, soda, or chocolate bars. I'm not a big fan of advertising, but I have to say that Brita and other water filters should be making way more money than Nestle per year. Those filters do a lot more for your water than anything being done by Nestle, Coke, or Pepsi.

…we'll be back after these commercials… Hey you! Do you ever have trouble telling if the toilet seat is open or closed?

Honey, where's the credit card? If I order a Bowl-Brite in the next three minutes, we get an extra one for the downstairs toilet! We can light up the toilets!

For only twelve payments of $14.95, you can keep the lights off while you urinate in the middle of the night. Even better, you can make your anus glow in the dark while you use the toilet. Can you say magical?

But WAIT! There's MORE!!

For just $1.75, you can buy a sparkling bottle of Nestle PureLife. Would you just look at it? It's no different than the water coming from your faucet, but it comes in this beautiful one-time use container. We gave some people in Maine $200 for a few billion dollars' worth of water. You need this, to support the people of Maine. For every dollar spent on Poland Spring water, we'll slap one baby in Fryeburg.

Aww, shit, hurry up with that card, hon! They're selling water in plastic bottles now! I didn't even know I needed that! What a wonderful world we're living in!

Aside from the water bottles, Rachel Carson and Earth Day did in fact change the country's behavior, if only microscopically. The U.S. and much of the world recognized that there was indeed a problem. The only places DDT is even discussed are parts of Asia and Africa, simply because there seems to be no solution to their malaria-ridden mosquitoes. They're forced to pick an evil.

The Environmental Protection Agency was established in 1971, and they directly attribute credit to Ms. Carson and *Silent Spring* for its creation. It was difficult to find many conversations about the environment before then, and the word "environment" had not even appeared in any U.S. legislature yet. She forced the world to discuss the world they were living in, which is inherently very strange. Humans lack of respect for the environment stems from the idea that we are separated from it, as if nature or the environment were some entity. We live within it; breathe its air, walk on its surfaces, eat and drink its bounties. Just because we can wear clothes and control the temperature in our homes does not mean we have exited the environment. You are nature, and every single thing you see is part of it as well.

It seems that most people just weren't aware of the immensity of those situations. They are *still* in the dark, and now the *Silent Spring* is screaming at the top of its fucking lungs. The birds are quiet because they wish the humans would just speak up for themselves. The *Lorax* is a fucking metaphor, he will not be popping out of a tree in the Congo.

Let's go through it again, hopefully for the last time. Change is possible, we've seen it happen; go throw your trash on the ground on Main Street. Someone will make sure you know how much of an asshole you are, and most people would agree.

Littering became a behavior deemed criminal, thanks to one of the only advertising campaigns worth watching, ever. Anyone who watched television in the 70s remembers "Iron-Eyes Cody", an Italian actor in a Native American costume stands on the side of the highway as a station wagon passes, hurling fast-food trash at him.

In his best fake Native American accent, he says, *"People start pollution, people can stop it."* He turns to face the camera with a tear streaking down his face. Fade to black. *"Get your copy of 71 ways to stop pollution... and help keep America beautiful."* We can only hope the commercial would have had hired a better casting director but still, it's cinematic wonder, for sure. Flippant nonsense.

Now I can call some person a litterbug and ostracize them. Some states offer hefty $2000 fines for littering. A friend of mine paid $250 for tossing a cigarette butt out of the car window. He paid his fine and stopped throwing his cigarettes out of the car; so, lesson learned, I suppose. Win a small one for the *Monkey Wrench Gang*.

No one seemed to want to address the contents of the trash thrown at that "Native American", the plastic utensils and containers or the disgusting food which the consumer didn't even finish eating. Maybe because it was entirely unsatisfying, or perhaps it was the result of a portion sized large enough for four adults. Even if the car had placed that stuff in a garbage can, it wouldn't have been properly handled.

The food in United States is treated as if were an endless resource. As far as this society can see, it is endless. The food wasted due to irresponsibility of every person capable of deciding what they want for dinner.

On farms, in grocery stores and restaurants, and in every home across America, 30-40% of all the food that is made is thrown into a landfill. It doesn't seem this way because all we can see is food everywhere, the waste is hidden. How can we be wasting almost half of all of the food if I can go shopping or get takeout right now?

These gigantic supermarkets fill too much space, and then work hard to keep that space full. They work hard to maintain a display which encourages you to buy more. It's hard to even find an empty spot in the orange display. This isn't because *nobody* is buying oranges, it is consistently rearranged for appearance after an orange is taken. The illusion of infinite resources.

America sees this as a form of progress, but it is quite the opposite. In most countries, a grocery store is no larger than a CVS.

They still carry all of the same ingredients, and they keep the shelves stocked. Our supermarkets use psychology to arrange the products to induce sales. We have massive grocery stores that are overfilled and most of the food is being wasted. The whole illusion exists for aesthetic beauty.

It was wonderful when human beings discovered they can work together in order to survive. A single person couldn't take down a wooly mammoth, but when a crew was assembled, they could work together to take it down and eat comfortably for weeks.

Then, some asshole, whom would probably work at DowDupont or Nestle today, suggested an even bigger idea. What if we chase twenty mammoths off of a cliff, wipe out the herd, and never hunt again? Our children won't even have to hunt!

The Seasons

It wouldn't be a stretch to say that most Americans have never even seen a farm in person, except for maybe their third-grade field trip. Does it matter? 90% of the U.S. population lives within ten miles of a Wal-Mart. Who needs farms? Gross. Cows, like, poop on the ground and stuff. I want to buy my Pringles and my shoes at the same store, damn it.

We need the farms, but they are also a large problem with food waste. Most of this is due to the tremendous demands for chicken and beef. Don't worry about the pork, we ship much of ours to Japan and what we eat comes from China. They have plenty for us, too- with their "hog hotels", huge structures as high as 13 stories with 1,000 pigs per floor. There are an infinite number of resources about this disturbing subject, you're all aware. I won't go there.

The fruits and vegetables are a serious problem as well. Almost 20% of harvests are often wasted. Some has to do with the stores and consumers strange cosmetic standards on fruits and vegetables. Most of us have no idea what celery really looks like because they cut half of it off and stick it in a bag for us. The grocery store isn't going to take an untrimmed celery plant with leaves. It probably wouldn't sell at the store anyways. It would be deemed ugly, removed from the shelf, and tossed in a dumpster in the back of the grocery store. Most Americans wouldn't know what to do with celery leaves, anyhow.

If you need some celebrity voice to make this all seem official, Anthony Bourdain made it simple, "Use everything, waste nothing." Your grandmother lived by this rule, and somewhere it was lost.

Most farms are just trying to fill demand and pay their bills, but Americans do not make normal demands. We have forgotten some simple things about almost all aspects of our food that are fundamental to our lives. It is hard to understand how much work goes into producing the food, or how much transportation is typically involved. Being so removed from the process of production, Americans are able to waste guiltlessly.

Fruits and vegetables grow in particular seasons. Is anyone aware of this anymore?

Maybe we just don't have the patience to flow with the seasons. Everyone gets excited about pumpkin flavored things in fall, and we've all seen the shift in advertising when the time comes around. Every product you can eat has been infused with pumpkin, from the coffee to the fucking Oreos.

This is because that's when pumpkins grow. During pumpkin season.

You should not be eating avocados in South Carolina in the middle of the fucking winter. You probably shouldn't even be eating an avocado if you're not in Florida, California, or Hawaii. The American desire for this stupid fruit developed at the same time people were telling them to shop local. Some really confused people were doing both at the same time.

California couldn't keep up with demand, so now we import unbelievable quantities from Mexico and Chile. Mexico's drug cartels are even trying to get it on the market. This is a brand-new enterprise. Ask your parents if they even knew what an avocado was when they were young.

Someone called it a *superfood* and even the most "environmentally friendly" people are consuming avocados daily, regardless of the time year. There are hipsters eating free-range chickens that incidentally forced twenty humans to work unrewarding jobs and deliver them an avocado across the country.

I wonder if my carrots get jet-lag?

If you think eating local is some sort of some sort of hippy shit, you are missing the point. This is the BEST possible way to eat food. It wasn't boxed and transported or frozen. It wasn't made in a machine. Nobody fucked with it. Sounds crazy, maybe even unbelievable, but it popped out of the Earth like a magnificent gift. Not to mention, if you're not going to care about the quality of your food, you may as well have the Deadhead at the market do it for you.

These are just small examples of the scandalous amount of resources wasted just to produce the food. That's not even the worst part. We could throw 75% of the food produced in the trash and still feed the same amount of people. The real problem is that all of this waste has nowhere to go, and landfills provide us with this illusion that everything is being handled.

Nobody is taking care of our waste. The recycling industry is meant for metals and cardboard, and much of the cardboard isn't recycled properly because of food residue or the chemicals used to add color. We only recycle about half of the cardboard, 25% of glass, and 30% of metals, which is another unnecessary addition to our dumps.

Only two states accept plastic water bottles for redemption. Some things like aluminum can be recycled over and over again. It's too bad only ten states have can and bottle redemption programs, especially considering the products exist all over the country. The states where the containers are made or filled don't even collect and recycle them.

Paper products find their way to landfills because of paper towels, napkins, etc., things that can often be recycled. I've worked through a few trees worth of paper towels just drying my hands, and unfortunately most of that paper product went in the trash. It will degrade, but it never needed to be in a landfill.

Regardless, plastic cannot be recycled more than once. 90% of the time, that singular recycle never even occurs. Many people would have no problem avoiding plastic where possible, if they were aware of this. The same applies to food. Most people haven't been made aware of the scandalous amount being thrown away, or the damage caused by wasting it.

One thing that came from all of the environmental attention raised in the 70s can be seen in the form of blue recycling bins. They made them of plastic, to collect your plastic. At least they tried, we'll give them a D for effort. One baby step at a time. Most places across the United States, businesses and homes alike, now regularly use a trash can *and* a recycle bin. It took a while, but it gained traction and became standard.

There needs to be a third bin, and some countries have already begun this practice. There needs to be an additional bin at every household, business, school, grocery store, and restaurant. We don't have time to start next year, it doesn't require much planning. Every single place there is a trash can, there should also be a recycling and food waste bin.

The food that goes uneaten is detrimental to the environment, which is silly because that's where it came from. By placing it in a landfill, we're just forcing it to stick around longer. It's also wasting a tremendous amount of money. Most of us can appreciate at least one of those things. Doesn't the United States want to be the world leader in all categories?

In the year 2020, some people have finally begun to consider where their food comes from. Now, we need to invest the same amount of thought into where it goes afterwards.

80,000,000,0000 pounds – just in case the word billion doesn't hit home hard enough. Look at all of those zeroes.

That is 30-40% of all the food being produced in the U.S.

The equivalent of roughly $161,000,000 per year.

Worldwide, the wasted food is estimated to be worth about $750,000,000,000 ($750 billion) per year. most of this money is wasted because of billions of lazy and selfish decisions.

This is in addition to the tremendous amount of landfill space occupied by this food, and the overwhelming amount of resources involved. 97% of the wasted food goes in a landfill. That's frightening, 10% would be concerning.

This means that during my short thirty years on this planet, my country has wasted about 2,400,000,000,000 pounds of food.

Two trillion, four hundred billion pounds of food, rotting in landfills with discarded shoes, microwaves, and pop-tart wrappers; despite the fact that most of it would have naturally decomposed, if only it weren't buried under assorted plastic garbage. Most of it should have just been eaten by any living animal or human anywhere.

For those who want to put money ahead of everything else, I can even support your lifestyle here. We'll make you some money, don't you worry. The United States always seems to be fretting gross domestic profit and other monetary status symbols. The amount of money wasted in thirty years, just by wasting food and mixing it in the garbage is $72 trillion.

Seventy-two trillion dollars wasted. Imagine setting $72,000,000,000,000 on fire. Even someone living off-grid in the middle of the woods in Maine would shudder at the sight of that. I don't think my mind is capable of imagining a pile of $72 trillion dollars. My bank account is usually less than $72, unless it's payday.

Being the world leader in waste is not an achievement. That means last place. The worst. How does this country feel about being the WORST at something? I said it, please, prove that the only reason is lack of knowledge.

They haven't covered it on the news enough, and the articles are boring and filled with statistics. Unfortunately, the people watching PBS are usually already aware of the issue. I guess *Sesame Street* leads straight to an ivory tower. It took my own experiences with food waste to start researching the numbers. I still don't believe them. While readily available on government websites, it was not easy to find many *conversations* about food waste.

Now, we will know and no longer can we turn a blind eye and pretend we don't know what we're doing.

Many countries have already implemented policies to curb food waste, but all of these actions are way too slow. The U.K. made some progress, reducing waste by 11% in three years.

In the U.S. few years ago, the EPA set a goal to reduce food waste by half in 2030. Is anyone even aware that this is happening? Do we begin in 2029?

The United States government is making hardly any effort. It's embarrassing. They're not alone, but that isn't an excuse. As my pops always said, *be a leader, not a follower.* The best part is, most of the world loves to imitate our culture and we are great at export.

San Fransisco and Seattle deserve their credit, of course. They already have garbage trucks that separate food waste. I haven't quite figured out why they seem be the only major cities aware of this problem. The state of California is passing laws banning the production of gasoline vehicles, but avoiding the easiest solution to methane gases and pollution.

California also seems to have passed some sort of regulation on recycling plastic recently, but they seem to be operating on the idea that plastic is recyclable. They should ban plastic, and watch the rest of the country follow suit. It may take some time, but we've got to try and avoid dragging out this recovery process.

In France, grocery stores face large fines for disposing of food that could be eaten. It's not a socialist plot to feed all of those that can't afford it. It's a simple redirection of what would have been wasted. Instead of throwing a dented apple away because no one will buy the thing, let the guy who hasn't eaten since Tuesday have at it.

South Korea has made efforts to become a zero-waste society, and they have directly addressed food waste. In 2013, their government passed a law that required food waste to be measured and deposited in a corresponding bin. A small fee is assessed for the amount of waste. The less you waste, the less it will cost you. Nobody wants to pay for their meal twice. It's quite simple, really.

I can even imagine my own father getting on board, shoving a spoonful of vegetables down my throat while screaming about Food Waste bills. *"You better clean that plate, I don't work sixty hours a week for you to throw food in the trash! I paid $7.75 last month for all your damn waste!"*

I can also imagine my father patriotically exclaiming, *"South Korea and France are beating us? Those snail-eating bastards we saved in WWII? They'd be speaking German if it weren't for us."*

Yes sir, along with those meat pie eatin', warm-beer drinkin' lobsters. It was a good idea to throw the tea in Boston harbor, but only then. Those of us alive now are just throwing our own food supply off of the boat because we arrived late to the party. It just looked like people were throwing everything in the water, so we joined in.

Whatever it takes, find your own personal reason for committing to remedy this terrible travesty.

For all of those with children, why do you hate them? I don't have kids of my own, but it seems kind of strange to hate your children so much that you would actively destroy their home.

The air we breathe, the oil we guzzle, the food we eat- it all comes from the planet.

I think some of us have forgotten. Food and oil appear like a gift from a wizard, that is unless you've worked in food service or driven through Texas and seen the endless oil wells chugging away.

I'm not trying to make everyone switch to automatic faucets or change your lightbulbs. I'm not even going to try to sell you anything. Of course, we all love that new sensation of automatic toilets flushing beneath you when you shift your weight. I know that Tesla cars are way overpriced, and most people think that a Prius just looks silly. Using less plastic is really easy, and many products have alternatives available. Companies will change with our purchases. I'm not sure what they'll put laundry detergent in. However, if they're smart enough to invent laundry detergent, they can create a container. We can figure these things out.

This isn't a message about finishing all of your food because there are starving kids somewhere. There certainly are starving kids everywhere, but we cannot even talk about them until we clean up our act, literally and metaphorically speaking. Actually, if we just clean up after ourselves, they can eat all of the wasted food our spoiled asses won't eat. Most of it is completely fresh and was thrown away because they didn't know what to do with it.

Just stop wasting food. If you don't care about the planet- your home- then you must not care about your children. We are actually facing a new possibility in the United States- **your children may very well live with a lower quality of life than their parents.** That doesn't sound like parental love to me.

Oh my, did he just say we hate our children? I'm not reading anymore of this. This book should be banned! I love my children, this is blasphemy!

Prove it.

The best part is- it is very simple. It costs nothing to stop wasting food the way that we do. It would create lots of jobs, some of the investors and moguls could even start businesses and be extremely profitable, just keeping food waste from ending up in landfills.

For years, RC Farms in Las Vegas was collecting 30 tons (60,000 lbs.) of wasted food per day to feed 6,000 pigs. This was a small operation, and although they took 30 tons a day, that was only about 8% of what Las Vegas was wasting. Those 24 hour all-you-can-eat buffets are wasting 540,000 per day. That's one microscopic example in one city, which is visited for the explicit purpose of being irresponsible.

Waste Management, the company mindlessly handling most of Americas trash, made almost $4 billion last year. Republic Services, their competitor, made $2.5 billion. There is already a market of almost $7 billion in waste, and they don't even do anything except bury it in the ground. Imagine all of the money to be made if it were done correctly.

Waste Management is like the *Ministry of Plenty* in *1984*. For those unfamiliar, the *Miniplenty* exists to ration resources and ensure that citizens do not have plenty of anything. In the same regard, Waste Management exists to ensure that your waste is not managed. They definitely provide a service- hiding the trash from the citizens who create it, *and for that, we thank them*. Well, not really. They're Billy Bob Thornton as your little league coach, "Rub some dirt on it."

Part of the problem is the belief in the "recycling industry." For example, I recently watched two documentaries about landfills and plastic. In the first, a woman working at a recycling plant in California gives a tour of a wonderful facility that separates materials by hand and really seems to care about recycling. She explains the process, and then says, "This is the plastics, we will be putting this on a barge to be shipped over to China, and they'll probably use it to make new things that we'll buy again." This seems like it makes sense, I like this lady.

In the next documentary, a man visits landfills and recycling plants in China. He discovers MOUNTAINS of unusable plastic. Rows of towers forming cities of mashed plastic bottles. The owner of the plant explains most of it is useless, made of plastic that cannot be recycled. Upon closer inspection of labels on the plastic, almost all of it is from California. Also, since the filming of that documentary, China has stopped importing plastic because they have no idea what to do with the shit we sent them.

Our society is being manipulated, and even some of the most environmentally-conscious citizens are unknowingly helping to perpetuate the lies. We need to take personal responsibility, because there is no one else paying attention.

For all of the corporations that *think* they will be negatively affected, you have the most wonderful public relations opportunity that has ever been. Your profits would only be affected temporarily, because if the companies involved with production were responsible for disposal- it would create so many new possibilities for money that I'm incapable of even listing all of them.

It makes logical sense. If we want to get elementary, remember what your fourth-grade science teacher taught you. *Each action has an equal and opposite reaction.* The daunting amount of food product being shipped to restaurants, schools, universities, retirement homes, and grocery stores daily has no escape route. It is dropped there, and responsibility for all of the containers and waste involved is displaced to the establishment itself, whom further displaces it to you and then to the local government, who probably has a contract with Republic Services or Waste Management. They dump it in the ground or into the ocean.

Not my chair, not my problem.

A whole chain of production and consumption filled with people expecting others to clean up after them. Picture this public service announcement:

We're DowDupont, and over the past year, we have collected 300 billion tons of plastic from the ocean and landfills across the world. With the help of our partners, Waste Management and Nestle, we have reduced the damage we caused to the planet for the sake of money. In the meantime, we created thousands of jobs and restored the populations of twelve endangered species! Without even trying, or really breaking the bank. Actually, our profits are beginning to rise with the opening of our new waste management plants. We still have a long way to go; will you join us?

That is an advertisement I would not skip, and probably the only positive public relations campaign in history. I'd even watch a corporate sponsored prime-time TV series about it. We can even combine it with the *Amazing Race* and call it a treasure hunt. Run around the world and clean some landfills.

Did you hear that, investors? The chance of a lifetime. *They've become the first corporation to actively engage in saving the planet!* Here are all of the government contracts, and all of the dollars.

The Volunteer

We got a thousand points of light
For the homeless man
We got a kinder, gentler machine gun hand
We got department stores and toilet paper
Got Styrofoam boxes for the ozone layer
Got a man of the people, says keep hope alive
Got fuel to burn, got roads to drive
-Neil Young- *Keep On Rockin' In The Free World*

Melissa has a freedom most of us wish we possessed. It wasn't always this way; she had worked at a grocery store through college. Immediately afterwards she overexerted herself in pursuit of the position of Produce Department Manager, working sixty hours a week. By the time she was thirty, she had risen to the General Manager position after her predecessor unexpectedly quit, and she had proven herself capable. Her degree in business was hardly relevant, but it had allowed her to apply for the position ahead of schedule, so it was of some use. She had cleaned toilets, dealt with spills, worked overtime, and suffered with most of us regular joes.

As a complete surprise, at thirty-two years old, her world was flipped upside down in the best way. Her underappreciated position that demanded almost eighty hours per week from her crumbling body was beginning to look like a major dead end. When her inheritance came around, her head was taken up off of the floor and she stood on her feet for the first time in a while. It felt like that first few weeks of college, the world was hers and she just needed to go collect what she was owed.

Now, she didn't have to work, her bills were always paid on time, and she could travel freely without applying for vacation days or pretending to be sick. There wasn't a more fantastic feeling in the world- pure liberation.

Growing up, her parents were very strict, and very cheap, which drove her insane. She enjoyed a very happy childhood, but she was never allowed to experience the common excesses of her peers. She had never chased an ice cream truck, her father would have never coughed up the quarter for that, unless maybe it were her birthday. Even then, he would do that thing where he strokes his chin, wondering how to let his child down with some complicated explanation about work and money that will go right over her head.

Family vacations happened once per year, and they were nothing more than a visit to her cousin's place two hours away. They did live right by a lake but this was never a proper vacation. The opportunity came when her friend's family was going to Disneyland for a week, they thought it would be nice to bring Melissa along. They had even offered to pay; her parents said it was no problem, it would be great to have a friend on the trip.

Her father had said that this was too much, he did not want to be indebted. He appreciated the offer but Melissa would be travelling with the family for their yearly vacation in just a few months. One vacation per year is plenty, he had said.

Her friend was nice enough to bring her back a park map and show her all of the wonderful rides that she was unable to try. She also made the effort to get a bunch of autographs from Mickey and the gang, but Melissa had tossed that in the trash with her hopes for a real vacation. She kept the park map, though she really didn't know why.

Melissa had loved her parents, but after college their interactions were limited to holidays and the occasional phone call. She supposed it would have been different if there were children to visit, but that was way out of the question. Deep down, she knew her parents resented this.

Melissa's mother passed away and her father retired from teaching. He was a professor at the women's college, a job which gave him more joy than anything else. He always had the love of his students. Many of them remained in contact with her father long after their graduation, right until his death. The service held for him was attended by nearly seven hundred people, mostly students.

Melissa knew her father was one of those rare teachers that students really appreciated because they had actually learned from him. Students want to learn but every teacher doesn't find a way to connect and deliver those nuggets of wisdom. We have all had that one teacher that got through whatever walls we had constructed, and we remember their names for decades after. For many students, this was Melissa's father.

In many ways it made her jealous. At home, her father was a great teacher but hardly exuded the love she wanted. He made a great college professor but if he were in a classroom with children, it's unlikely they would learn a thing. He just couldn't connect with children, and he didn't find it necessary. It was as if he waited for her to grow up, before he began to interact. By then it was too late. It had created a relationship with no foundation, and she wished she could have connected with her father like his students had claimed.

Her mild resentment for her father's parental downfalls were forgiven on the day that he died. It wasn't long after her mother, and the family knew this would happen. He was like a helpless puppy without her- incapable of cooking or cleaning because he never had to learn. He was an intelligent man, but he lived in the academic world.

Three months after her mother passed, Melissa's father followed. She was hurt, and she grieved terribly for weeks. Her thoughts were continuously lost in memories she analyzed thoroughly. Melissa had never wondered before, if she had loved them enough or shown her immense appreciation. Losing them felt like a failure, as if she had not done enough yet to prove herself worthy of their love before they left this world.

It was hard for her to mourn, though, having been completely liberated from all of her stresses. Her penny-pinching father had managed to accumulate quite a sum of money, being a professor for forty-two years and keeping kids from free Disneyland trips.

She would never forget the conversation which changed her life.

"Ms. Detrick, your father has left the deed to the house in Wellesley in your name. He has requested that you honor him by donating his library to the university. He wrote, "It can be anonymous, but a little plaque would be nice. With the amount of time I put in there, I deserve a wing in my name.""

He has also written the following, "My little cub, I know how you feel about my Mustang in the garage. I only ask that you find an owner who will love my other baby girl for all that she is worth. Find someone who needs the car and will show it the love and respect it deserves. Give it away, I don't care, as long as the person is worthy."

Melissa almost jumped from her chair. "He wants me to give away a car that is probably worth at least $500,000? And that's a low estimate! Do you know he is talking about a *1967 Shelby GT500 Mustang?* Do you have any idea what that car means to a collector? I hate the thing, because he wasted more time working on it than he did with me. It was like he used it to escape from the house, and that made me hate that stupid car. I'll be damned if I do anything but sell it for every penny I can get."

"Ms. Detrick, it's not my place to say, but I don't think you'll need that money, after you've seen the amount of money in your father's estate. The money he hoarded through the years was invested wisely and strategically. He has left you a sum in the amount of $3.4 million dollars, and he only asks that a small portion be donated to the university in his honor."

"That's not funny. $3.4 million dollars? My father drove the same station wagon for twenty-three years and re-used his tea bags!"

"Well, it appears that he had done that for a reason. I have dealt with many cases; most do not end in joy like yours. Many people lose a family member and end up stuck with bills to pay, messes to clean. Your father was different, he seemed to be focused on the future his entire life. Your father once told me he always ate lunch at the university, even on days off."

"Yeah, breakfast and lunch! And at least once a week, that was where my dinner came from! He was cheaper than cheap, and he was very inventive. I remember when the lawnmower broke, and he rigged it up with an engine from a broken- down speedboat at my cousin's lake. I had to ride home with that hunk of metal in the back of our wagon. The thing was loud as hell and it hardly even did the job. I can't believe that was all happening with his pockets loaded. I was the one who had to mow the frickin' lawn."

"Well, the money's now yours. Sign here, agreeing to his conditions, and the money will be transferred within the next week. Good luck, Ms. Detrick."

It was overwhelming at first, living without a schedule or any responsibilities. After a few months of vacations and living the high life, Melissa settled into her new existence with comfort. She even got herself a yearly membership to Disneyland. She may have been more excited than a girl dressed like *Cinderella* eating breakfast with Cinderella in her castle.

After she had cruised the 101 in her Mustang a few times and worn out Disneyland, she began spending each day walking in the nearby park, just observing the environment around her. It seemed that she had never paid much attention to anything before. She was beginning to notice an unfamiliar world.

While sitting on a bench and reading a book, Melissa heard a dog bark twice. She didn't see a single person in sight and even after walking in the direction of the bark, she couldn't find the dog.

After a few minutes of curious searching in silence, the dog barked again, revealing itself by the bushes at the edge of the park. She decided to see if it had been left alone and needed help. She approached and cautiously extended her hand. He gave it a sniff with a playful bark and she followed his leash to the bushes. With no one in sight, she figured she should help the dog somehow.

Melissa reached into the bush and felt a leg.

"…the fuck you doin'?" A voice exclaimed from pile of raggedy gray clothes in the bush.

Melissa jumped right out of her skin and her heart sink like an anvil. The man had scared the life out of her; unintentionally managing to make her feel like the worst person in the world.

"I'm so sorry, I thought…I thought the dog was left here by somebody…" She walked away quickly, hiding her face in remorse, wondering what could be done. She had to leave the situation; her emotions were nothing but a confusing haze.

After she sat in her car for a few minutes, Melissa realized she had to do something for the man, even if it were to buy him a six-pack of beer to forget his troubles. She walked back over to the bush, only to find that the man had gone. She walked in search of him and found nothing.

She returned to the park each day as she had been, but it was weeks before she had seen him again. When he came to the park on a foggy morning, he hardly expected to have to deal with helping Melissa heal her emotional scars. Scars caused by the mere sight of him.

"Can I grab you a cup of coffee? Are you hungry? Is he hungry, what's his name?" She asked, reaching down to pet the dog, and he embraced it with all of the love a dog can give.

"This is Faulkner. He's almost deaf, but he's got plenty of love. Been with me since the days I had a house. He don't mind, I think he just misses that old recliner chair, don't ya, boy?"

The two of them went to the nearest coffee shop, and despite the snarling looks of the employees and customers, Melissa and a new friend named Rich enjoyed a cup of coffee.

"How long have you been on the streets? If you don't mind me asking. I'm sorry, is that rude?" Melissa immediately regretted the question.

"It ain't rude, hon. How could you not wonder how I got to be this way? I used to wonder how it happened to the others, when I was living good. Then it happened to me. It took some time, but it seems like I woke up one day and lost everything.

I worked in the same factory that my father had worked in for 37 years. I had been there for twelve years myself, and during my time the place was transformed. More machines led to less jobs, and then when 500 employees became 100, the owner sold it off. They told us we would remain employed but that didn't last long. Plus, they took away all of our benefits and cut our hours. It dwindled until they finally came in one day and told us it was all over. The factory was closing.

I collected unemployment for a while, and my wife went back to work. I couldn't find a new job though, not many factories left like that. I found odd jobs, and even drove a limousine for a while. Couldn't get hired full-time anywhere. Unemployment ended, and the debt buried me. We lived a comfortable life of middle class, and we never expected it to end. The debt we had accumulated could only be managed with the job I had.

My wonderful marriage to the woman I loved became a dueling match fueled by dollar bills. We argued about everything and we experienced the real power of money, when you don't have any. We lost our love, and she moved in with her sister.

I stayed, tried to save the house and find work, hopefully restore my marriage. It took six months for me to lose the house, and I took to the streets in my car, loaded with as many possessions as possible. I sold each and every item, right down to the car. Shoulda waited 'til winter was over for that one, but me and the pup were starving.

Here I am today, drinking coffee with you. Wondering if this is all some sort of nightmare that has kept me asleep for the past six years. Maybe I fell in the kitchen and now I'm comatose. Wake me up, would ya!" He shook his fist at the sky. He always had to end the story with a joke, for he had told it so many times that the reaction of watching someone's heart break for him, disintegrated his own broken heart.

That's how long we've been out here- six years. This guy used to fit in my pocket back then. But we're doing alright, ain't we boy? I've got my best friend, and the food bank helps us out sometimes."

"What do you mean, sometimes?"

"Aww, well, they usually run out of food by the afternoon, they only have so much. Sometimes, I let the others eat and just get their bones for Faulky. He could eat all day long, if we had the means. I just can't bring myself to fill a plate when I see the children come in. They can eat two helpings before I have mine, no doubt about that. Those women that work at the food bank really try though, bless their hearts. They just don't have the funds, and there are twice as many plates to be filled as six years ago."

"That's the craziest thing I have ever heard. Guess what, Rich? My dear old dad has some food for you. I can't think of a better way to spend some money. Let's take a ride down to this food bank. First, let's hit the grocery store. I can't save everybody but I can at least afford to get enough for the day."

That meeting with Rich had taken place almost three years ago. She dove headfirst into the battle to save the food bank and began spending her days begging and pleading with the community for a little help. These years of generosity were beginning to have a serious impact on her savings. She didn't mind spending the money, but she was acutely aware that if she kept on spending this way, she would have to go back to work within five years. The very thought made her cringe. A meaningless job with no emotional reward for a meager paycheck. At least the food bank allowed her to take part in something bigger than herself. Though recently she had found herself hopelessly harassing the town for food donations, at least that's how she felt.

Entering yet another restaurant, Melissa feels that hanging sense of sadness that plagues her daily. Being forced to beg a business for their food scrap is not the most dignified experience. Each restaurant felt worse than the last, but today she would finally stumble into my place of employment.

She had come before my dinner shift, so I had missed their discussion of donating food. Thankfully, my partner in crime was on shift and paying attention. Otherwise, I never would have met *sweet Melissa.*

Wally ran the grill when I wasn't there, and we didn't often get to work together. The two of us got along too well, and the boss separated us like fourth graders. We didn't mind having all of the available morning shifts though, that's for sure.

The morning often brings vendors trying to sell their products to restaurants. Companies and farms send representatives with samples and the cooks try them out. The manager says, "Sure, I'll give you a call," and we never hear of that food again. In fifteen years, I never witnessed one of these vendors make a sale.

Wally always made sure to avoid these salesmen. Never even says hello, just gives them a nod and grabs the manager. *Ain't nobody got time for that.*

"There's someone here to see you, asked for a manager. I'm not sure who they are"

"Well, why didn't you ask?" The manager rolled his eyes and made his way to the dining room where a woman stood waiting. She was a lot easier on the eyes than the food salesmen. Some might even call her beautiful, though she really couldn't care less.

"Hi there! I'm Melissa, I'm from the food bank down the street… I was just stopping by all of the local restaurants to see if there is anything you frequently throw out at night, that could be donated? We're looking for anything, really, we've had some funding problems and any help at all would be great… The café down the street is even going to give us their bread ends to make bread pudding. Really, anything."

She stood in the dark dining room alone, appearing tiny beneath the towering chairs resting on the tables. The manager flipped the lights on in the dining room and he hesitated, dreading this situation. It had happened before, and it would happen again.

With a sigh, he let out, "I'm really sorry, but we're not allowed to donate any of leftover food. It's a legal thing, we could face lawsuits. I really wish I could, but it could get us in big trouble."

"I understand. Let me give you my information in case anything changes," she remotely replied. She had heard this before, and it is likely she would hear it ten more times today, but she had to keep trying.

She found herself feeling empathy for telemarketers, of all people. They don't want to call you, but they won't be paid otherwise. If Melissa doesn't beg for food she will spend her own money to ensure that they are fed. Tomorrow, the cycle begins anew.

The government funding had ended three weeks ago, after she had battled for almost a year beforehand to avoid it. The funding had come in a bill attached to many state programs, some of which had now been deemed unworthy. *Can't be spending money to teach kids the damn oboe, can we now?* The politicians had heard her pleas but claimed it would require an entirely new bill to maintain funding.

"I feel so bad, I wish I could have done something," the manager meaninglessly stated as he re-entered the kitchen. He had to make sure everyone understood that he really was a good guy. "This is like the third time this year someone has come asking for donations, and we throw out so much food."

"Wait… you told her we couldn't give her any food? We throw out a trashcan full of prepared stuff every single night," Wally chimed in from the back, storming forward. "I'll take it there myself."

"We can't do that. It's illegal, we could get in a lot of trouble."

"Who the fuck told you that? That is the biggest bunch of bullshit I have ever heard. Seriously, where did you hear that?"

"Dude, I've dealt with this before. Jay dealt with it when he was the GM here, and he said the same thing. Now, he's the district manager and I know he would say it again."

"Look at this, asshole," he let out, handing him his phone. His mother had always said, "If you have nothing to say, don't say anything at all." At this moment, calling the guy an asshole *was* the nice thing he could say.

The Bill Emerson Good Samaritan Food Donation Act

- The Federal Bill Emerson Good Samaritan Food Donation Act protects donor and the recipient agency against liability, excepting only gross negligence and/or intentional misconduct. In addition, each state has pas Good Samaritan Laws that provide liability protection to good faith dono

"Damn. I feel like a dumbass, I've gotta call Jay. He was always pissed that he had to throw food away," he turned to give back the phone. "Where did Wally go?"

"He just ran out the back door."

"Excuse me! Wait a second!" Wally screamed, as he caught up to the woman from the food bank. "Sorry… out of…breath… the manager…is an idiot… I am closing tonight, please come by around 11:15, or I can come by the food bank when I am done. I throw away lots of food every night. Are you from the one right down the street?"

"Yes, thank you so much! I'm Melissa, what's your name? How did you convince your manager?" Melissa was in disbelief.

"I'm Wally. I didn't convince him of anything, he just does anything he is told. It's requirement number one, to be a manager. Do you have your phone?"

"Of course, yes. Here, put your number in…"

"No, it's not for that. Well, I'll put my number in there, in case we are running late tonight or something," he put his number into her phone and handed it back. "I ask because… you should search for the "Good Samaritan Food Donation Act" and have the page ready. Do not let another manager tell you that donating food is illegal. Go tell the grocery stores, too. They toss better food than the restaurants."

Melissa floated off on air with a new sense of hope. This new bit of information was the weapon she needed, and it empowered her. At the same time, she felt depressed, remembering how many restaurants and grocery stores had *specifically* mentioned that they would not donate because they were afraid of lawsuits or losing their job. She'll be back for them.

She immediately took to the phone, hearing her father's echo in her head. *The pen is mightier than the sword.* He spent his days reading the words eschewed from other's pens, away from any possibility of proverbial swords.

"*Daily Mirror*, how can I help you?"

"Hi, my name is Melissa Detrick, I was hoping to place an ad on behalf of the Greene Street Food Bank. Well, really on behalf of everybody in this town and beyond."

"Let's see what we can do for you, I'm sure we'll make something happen. What were you looking to print?"

"Well, we lost our funding recently and we are in desperate need of donation. I have been to all of the local grocery stores; I've even asking local restaurants for scraps. So many of these places told me the same story…they don't want a lawsuit, lose their job…and so on. Someone could get sick from the food; they can't be responsible, blah, blah. I am surrounded by people waiting desperately for their next meal, it's heartbreaking. I spend my own money when I have to, but I can't keep that up forever. I shouldn't have to, either."

"I never understood that law, is it better to be sick from some food or starving? I don't rightly know, but I think I'd take the food," he sat distracted, trying to find a way to help the poor, selfless woman.

"That's the problem…when I was over at Johnny's, right by the Food Bank; one of the cooks showed me a law that actually says the exact opposite. The law about donating food isn't true. It's called the Good…Samaritan Donation Law… one second, I have it written down.”

He typed it into the search bar and received a few million results. There it was, summarized in plain English for the entire world to ignore.

“Holy shit! Woah sorry. I just found it on a Feeding America website. The Bill Emerson Food Donation Law? 1996?!?!”

“Yeah, I have been at this food bank for three years and I had no idea. I feel stupid. Is there any possible way to get this on the front page? I really just want to make everyone aware, even if it is the local paper.”

“Do not feel stupid. I worked at a grocery store when I was a teenager. We used to toss out full boxes of vegetables weekly for a variety of stupid reasons. It looked fine to me, almost every time. Always pissed me off, especially when I was young and idealistic. I used to ride my bike past a starving homeless guy on my way to that grocery store. He could have eaten like a king every day. There was one night I had to toss a hundred frozen pizzas out, I think there was some mistake with the stock and we had to empty an entire fridge.

I told him the homeless guy to go check the dumpsters, even if he couldn’t cook the damn things, he could have had some cold pizza. The dumpsters were locked at night, and I came in for my shift at 5 am to the poor guy sleeping, leaned up against the huge dumpster full of pizza. Just smelling the possibility of enjoying something that everyone loves and takes for granted- even if it was cold. I’ll never forget arriving to work on my bike that next morning.

From across the parking lot, I spotted his body propped up against the bright blue dumpster. My heart sank but that wasn’t even the worst part. When I reached the dumpster and took a look down, his knuckles were crusted with blood because he had been trying to pry his way into the dumpster for that pizza. Imagining him fighting this battle he never ultimately won made me feel like I belonged in the dumpster myself. I wanted to climb in the dumpster with that pizza and rot away.

The boss always said, "Nothing we can do, we could get in big trouble."

He continued without skipping a beat, "I'm sorry miss, I've been rambling. You're the first call I've taken in four days. Anyways, you don't need an advertisement. This is a story. I am going to put you through to somebody, stay on the line please. Melissa was your name? Hold on, hold on."

Melissa was blown away by this man's casually to pouring every detail of his life. She had clearly lit some sort of fire under him and his passion oozed through the phone. Melissa sat in a state of confusion, nostalgic for a time before she was born. Bach played through what sounded like she set the receiver next to a gramophone, full of static.

"This is Simon, what can I do for you?"

"Hi Simon, my name is Melissa…someone from the advertising department forwarded me to you… he was a very excitable man, said something like, *You don't need an ad, this is a story*. I was just looking to see if someone could help get the word out somehow…I manage the Greene Street Food Bank down town. We're just in desperate need of donations. I floated the idea of publishing on the front page, I have the money for it. Will the paper allow that?"

"Well, not even I get to say what goes on the front page. Well, sometimes, actually," he laughed. "Mostly, I just have to write a story out and hope that its deemed worthy of being there. Won't be cheap, I can tell you that. No one's ever asked before.

Do you have a story? The receptionist just handed me this note that says, "Good Samaritan Food Donation Act" and told me you were on line one. Usually, they tell me who's on the other end. He was acting weird. Give me a second…"

It took three seconds for an abrupt return to the phone, "Melissa, are you busy today? Can we grab a cup of coffee and talk?"

Bread and Circus

Here we go, another day in this dump. It wouldn't be long until the place was overwhelmed with the screaming of frantic cooks and waitstaff. The joy of silence ends with a doorbell ringing in the back. The circus begins.

"What's this doing here?"

"Well hello to you, too. I don't know, the delivery was made before I got here this morning. I saw the truck pulling away as I walked up," I replied, knowing this was the key to start the day off wrong. They should not have been here for at least another hour, no one was here to open the door for them. They left all of the food on the cement where the cooks smoke and spit, in back of the restaurant.

"Well that's nice. Blue cheese, ranch dressing…. oh! The sliced cheese, too. American, Swiss, Monterey Jack…. Got some lettuce here…. tomatoes…. celery…two boxes of chicken breasts. Nice. Straight to the dumpster, I'm not risking it," he began tossing the full boxes toward the back door, naming each item and the corresponding menu item as he let it fly. It really didn't make a difference that I had seen the truck leave, and the ingredients were only outside of the fridge for 30 minutes, at most. Not one ingredient could have possibly expired, but it was outside and unattended for thirty minutes. He just kept on rifling through and trashing the stuff.

"Guac, Cilantro. No quesadillas this week, I guess. Fuckin' assholes. 86 the menu. Damn drivers just threw all of this stuff outside of the fridge, are you kidding me? Now I've got to sit on the phone and try to get another delivery before Wednesday," he began dialing the phone and stormed outside.

I finished my prep and readied myself for the day ahead. In two hours, working alone, I've already filled two trash cans with plastic wrap, gallon-sized ranch containers, and the food left uncovered overnight. The restaurant isn't even open yet. Guess I'll take the bins out and get some air before the doors open. The dumpster is already overflowing from the week, and it reeks like a cesspool. It won't be picked up for three more days.

Did you make sure to rinse your yogurt cup and put it in the recycle bin? It doesn't matter, because I've just thrown six plastic containers the size of basketballs directly into a trash bag. Giant, dirty plastic containers mixed right in with some old soup, and a batch of thirty cheeseburgers that turned grey.

Most restaurants have a bin for cardboard, and a bin for trash. They do not recycle plastic. Maybe they know it wouldn't actually be recycled, but I doubt that. Ask your favorite restaurant. I've asked several owners at restaurants where I worked. The cost to have plastic recycling collected is too expensive. Everything goes in the trash bin; even worse, a quarter of the cardboard goes with it because it's lined with plastic to contain chicken blood.

I've argued that recycling would reduce the number of trash collections, therefore the price would balance out. Apparently, it still wouldn't make recycling cost-effective.

They give other nonsense reasons for objection, and throughout my time in twenty-plus restaurants, I had only seen two businesses recycle plastic and glass. Both of them were hipster or vegetarian places that actively considered the environment. They also composted, another thing I have never seen in any other restaurant.

Before the place has even opened, and one tiny restaurant in a small suburban city has already produced an amount of waste equivalent to that of two families of five over a few weeks. Just wait until I start cooking and throwing away fries.

As we open the doors, the usual rush comes- the ones that strongly reinforce my thought that there are many people incapable of cooking at all. The dumbass regular who doesn't seem to have anywhere to be, seemingly ever, storms in before the staff can even prop the door open with one of those little wedges. He arrived in the parking lot at 11:55 am, and at 11:59 he stood in front of the door.

He calls the waitresses by name, like it's some 50s diner in a movie.

Jess has asked the man several times to call her Jess, because no one calls her Jessie. Reminds her of her creepy stepdad. He doesn't care. They all cringe and wonder who gets stuck with the guy that comes in daily and never tips.

He actually claimed visiting daily as the reason, when a waitress overheard him telling a friend, "I come here every day, if I left a tip every time, it'd be like $50 a week!"

Of course, that means you should never leave a tip. You didn't occupy a table, or waste the waitresses and cooks time as you sat at the table for an hour with a freakin' grilled cheese and a Pabst Blue Ribbon? The man is one of the prime examples of a cog in the proverbial wheel. A menace to societal order, annihilator of customary behavior and unwritten rules. He has spent so much time in this restaurant that he actually believes the waitresses like him, thinks they're friends. Do you tip your friends?

They probably would enjoy his ridiculous behavior if he had left a tip, but he had never done so, not once. Each day he kicked through the door like Kramer and ordered up two pieces of cheese between bread.

The restaurant came to know him, unlovingly so, as the *Grilled Cheese Fucker*. He may or may not have had relations with the sandwich, I'm not one to say. It made us feel better to imagine that he did. All I know is, this lazy asshole came in every single day (except Sunday, that was reserved for Jesus) and paid $11.49 for a grilled cheese with fries and a 12-ounce beer.

A 6-pack of Pabst costs $4.50 plus deposit, even cheaper in most places. We'll call it five bucks. A loaf of bread will run you around $2. You'll get about ten sandwiches with that. Some cheese will cost $4 for a pound, likely enough for twenty grilled cheese sandwiches. Grab a bag of Ore-Ida for $4, and that's $15.00. Hardly more than one sandwich, a few fries, and one beer at the restaurant. With one trip to the grocery store, you would have enough to make six of these pathetic meals at home, with bread, fries, and cheese leftover.

At that price, each sandwich and beer- made with the same Land-O-Lake's American cheese and generic white bread, served with the same exact beer, would cost a tiny fraction of the daily price spent at this restaurant which offers no "experience" or specials, no wonderful ingredients unavailable to the masses. The waitresses do not flirt with him or offer any special treatment that would justify his daily visits. They hate him, actually.

Have you seen this, have you heard about this? Did everyone see Land-O-Lake's new logo? They got rid of the Native American and kept the land. Classy.

The Grilled Cheese Fucker is just accustomed to being waited upon and served. He probably lived in his mother's basement until he was forty; then she passed on and he was left to fend for himself. The restaurant food is simply made for him and served on a plate that he will not have to clean. The amount of energy wasted on a grilled cheese is exponential. The laziness is unbelievable.

I begin each day, finding myself irritated by grilled cheese. Admittedly, after fifteen years, I'm like that old teacher that has come to hate children but just won't retire. Fifteen years is way too long to be in the food service industry.

The grilled cheese is on the menu for picky children, not stupid adults. Philosophically, it pains me to know that some idiot ordering a grilled cheese could affect my mood, but I can't control it. What's sadder- it happens twice a week. The ticket starts making that nightmare printing sound, and I can't help myself from exclaiming, *Grilled cheese fucker!*

The man is an example of an industry that has blown itself way out of proportion. Eating out should be an experience, reserved for situations that demand it. Once-a-week at most, even just special occasions. It's understandable that dating and business often require these social interactions but it's crazy for each American city to have competing restaurants providing the same things you can buy at the supermarket.

Truthfully, when your local restaurant runs out of an ingredient that they need for a popular menu item, they will send the dishwasher to the grocery store to buy enough to get through the day. I have made many of these trips. Your result is a frozen, haphazardly assembled meal cooked by a person who just wants to go home and stop listening to the damn ticket machine.

There is no need for an adult to be visiting a restaurant daily for a grilled cheese. There is really no need to visit restaurants daily. Owners like regulars for business, your laziness pays their bills. The rest of us employees wonder what's gone wrong to make you this way.

I have also made peanut butter and jelly for an adult in a restaurant. It was one of the low points of my life, go ahead and call me dramatic. I was twenty-five years old, fresh out of college with the world ahead of me. Yet I found myself making lunch for imbeciles, spreading peanut butter and jelly on processed bread.

Most restaurant food isn't purchased because the restaurant has unique ingredients, an amazing chef, or even some tacky gimmick like *Shenaniganz*. Most restaurants exist simply to provide for a demand that perseveres because cooking requires effort and time. It's much easier to outsource those demands- cooking, cleaning, disposing.

Gee willikers, Batman! You can even get it to go and just eat it on the way to your next stop. Pop by the restaurant, eat the food, throw the container in the trash, and move on with the day. If you're down with the fast food, you don't even need to leave your freakin' car!

This must be the eighth wonder of the world. Forget that wall in China; I can drive right up to this here window and grab myself a sandwich before John Bonham strikes the drums in *Stairway to Heaven*. *...And as we wind on* down *the road...*

These are the things I wonder about, as I prepare grilled cheese for incompetents. Before I can brace myself for the show, the restaurant fills, and the orders begin spitting from the machine. The insane mental gymnastics are impressive if you can remember any of it afterwards. I managed to transcribe a small bit. Despite the overwhelming amount of nonsense being spoken, the following took place in a few minutes during a lunch rush.

"Walking in... two burgs- one double, one triple... LTO on the double, just American on the triple. Two Phillies walkin' in, one no pepper."

"Got it, heard," I reply quickly, and in my mind, the wheel spins erratically, but with direction. Flip these three burgers, get the crab out of the steamer and throw in the macaroni and cheese. Drop some fries and get cheese on the burger that's almost done. Oh shit, it's supposed to be Swiss cheese, not American. Damn, I have no

Swiss cheese. Gotta go to the walk-in. I need celery, too. I've still got to put down buns for…"

The machine starts to print again.

Walking in… three burgers- all doubles with American. All day- six burgers, two Phillies- one no pepper, one no cheese; three grilled chick sandies; and a snow crab. Need a mac and cheese from you, too. Is that snow crab up now?

Fry- all day- 10 fries, 4 kid's tenders, 3 Beantown plates, 3 buff shrimp, and a fish taco.

Heard.

Can someone empty our trashcans?

Got it.

Heard.

Fire 62!

Fish taco's up, plating now.

Straight to the window. Can someone drop two baskets of fries?

Heard.

How long on the first two kids' tenders?

Three minutes.

Two minutes on snow crab. Out of swiss, though, 86 it.

"*86 SWISS CHEESE!!*" he screams, as if I couldn't have done that myself. I meant write it on the damn board, so everyone is aware we are out of swiss cheese.

I forgot those chicken breasts were under the grill dome. Gotta flip those. What did I need, celery? I've gotta cheese these first two burgers and get the buns off the grill.

How long on the Swiss burger?

Shit, that's what it was. Swiss cheese. One minute, gotta grab more Swiss. Wait, what? There is no swiss.

Just put American, get the ticket out.

Heard.

Here come the waitresses- we can always count on them asking questions in the service window while we're doing twenty things.

Can I get that salad, please? It's been twelve minutes since I asked for that remake. How hard is it to throw lettuce and dressing in a bowl?

"I forgot about it, because there's no ticket. How hard is it to take an order and ring it in correctly the first time?"

Did you drop those fucking baskets of fries? I need fries, now. Make it three baskets.

My bad, three baskets heard.

Walking in- two tender plates, triple burger just pjack and mayo. Wait on the burger- going with wings. Fry- drop me 48 wings.

"I need a ranch and a bowl of chili with extra cheese on it, guy said triple it up on cheese if you can. He comes in all the time-the dude who gets the burger with butter," the waitress asserted as if she were telling us about a dear friend. I've got a list of tickets with thirty dishes to make, please, tell me about each one's life story and how often they visit our establishment.

I plate the crab and two sandwiches, then turn back to the grill.

These snow crab legs are all broken. Get me a new order on the fly.

"The box is like three-quarters full, almost all of them are broken. I made it work, they got more than three claws worth."

"Look like shit. Just open that new box. Toss the broken one. Walking in- two Phillies, straight-up. Medium burger on Texas with swiss, well-done burger with American"

"I just 86ed swiss, can you write it on the fucking board please? And are you sure about tossing this snow crab, the box is almost full?"

"Fuck it, this happens all of the time. I don't have time to pick through it for a couple of good ones. Toss it. Open the new box and throw a new order down.*"*

If it isn't obvious by now, I'm cooking dinner for a restaurant full of people at the same exact time. If you asked me immediately afterwards what I had just cooked, I couldn't tell you. I did my best to make it look appealing and taste well, but I'm working with frozen ingredients. Aside from burning it, I really have no control over the food.

I threw the fifty-pound box of snow crab to the back door, and it was thrown into the dumpster later. This happens regularly with any frozen item that has pieces, like shrimp, onion rings or mozzarella sticks. Nearly every time, at least 1/3 of every box are thrown away because they are broken into bits. Much of the time the box is in little pieces before even opened at the restaurant.

The amount of time wasted fishing, packaging, transporting, repackaging, transporting again, storing, and then transporting one more time, to be dumped in a landfill.... It's pretty tremendous. We produce almost twice as much food as we need for no reason at all.

The National Resources Defense Council actually made a PSA commercial that showed the life of a strawberry- from one side of the country to the other, picked from the plant specially to wind up in the trash.

For some reason, eating local has become a niche thing that only hipsters take part in, but this doesn't make any sense. Eating local is the best possible way you can purchase food. Envision something more sensitive than a strawberry. For example, a chicken wing.

I will leave out the gory details of raising chickens. The condition of chicken farms is only one of the many factors that should drive consumers to buy from somewhere local.

An old neighbor of mine consistently had ten chickens, he spent his days in the yard with them. He ate every single one, and he told me once that he eats eggs or chicken for nearly all of his meals. When I eventually had a taste, I thought he was messing with me. It did not taste like chicken; it was absolutely delicious with no spices, just a bit of olive oil. The guy even seemed to mourn for the creatures. I confusedly devoured a plate of chicken. When I finished, he took me outside and just pointed at two apple trees surrounded by happy birds.

"I don't feed them. Well, I take an apple picking trip here and there if I need to, but these things just eat all the apples on the ground. Sometimes they even hop on that branch and pick 'em right off. They eat the whole thing, core and all. Makes my life easy, and my terrible diet delicious."

Here is a little background on chicken wings.

Until 1964, absolutely no one ate the wings of a chicken. Have you looked at them? Cat food. Humans have opposable thumbs and think enough to give ourselves names, we can do better. When we eat meat, we are eating the muscles of the animal. With pork and beef, there are many different ways to cut the meat, which creates a variety of ways to serve. Filet, ground beef, steak, etc. The better the condition of the muscle, the better the meat. Waste aside, this is a benefit of free-range or grazing animals. They were actually allowed to use their muscles.

Chickens cannot fly. Their wings are pathetic, but there are entire restaurants in the United States based on serving up these tiny T-Rex things. The meat is so scarce that we practically have to suck it off of the bone. Somehow this trend has persevered through sixty years and is still going strong.

A woman who owned a restaurant in Buffalo, New York had received an accidental shipment of chicken scraps and had to make do. She picked out the wings, snapped them in half, and it's safe to assume she breaded and sauced them to disguise the fact that she was serving shit. Actually, the traditional way is to smother the wings in butter.

They still disguise it, why do you think Buffalo Wild Wings and other places of its kind have thirty flavors of sauces? Order a plain one, it is gross. Why are we eating these things? You can put breading on almost anything and add those sauces.

At just one of these restaurants, a chicken delivery includes a few hundred pounds of chicken wings. They come in huge boxes lined with plastic bags. At most restaurants in Massachusetts, the chicken came from Iowa, despite there being millions of chicken farms between those states. In this case, the reason for that distance is likely the amount of chicken being demanded at our restaurant. Mass produced without an ounce of care.

An egg is laid straight into a box, then placed in a gigantic incubator that can handle 60,000 eggs at one time. The eggs are moved along a conveyor belt, and a machine scans them, removing defects. The eggs are usually injected with antibiotics, then moved to another incubator. The eggs hatch, and the chicks are piled into boxes by the hundreds, poured into a machine. At egg farms, many males are separated and thrown in a blender, they serve no purpose there. The machine spits the useful chicks out into a truck as they are checked for disease, after which they taken to a farm which will raise them.

They are placed in a warehouse, or *raising room*, the floor of which is covered in wood chips to collect their urine and waste. They will spend three or four months in the warehouse, after which they will be slaughtered and separated into breasts, wings, legs, etc. by another machine. A few hundred wings are spit into a plastic bag, frozen for a few months, placed in a refrigerated truck, driven across the country, frozen again, thawed, cooked, and served. As far as food goes, this is the bottom of the barrel. In many cases, the wings were frozen for longer than the bird actually lived. There is an incomprehensible amount of ways food can be mistreated, and it becomes more likely when we nearly remove human beings from the equation.

To open a bag of wings floating in blood is pretty gross, it would make a lot of people vegetarians. I've seen some real disgusting stuff, but I'll treat this passage like a newscast and interrupt with a positive story. *After the break: A fifth of the Amazon is gone, and 80% of it is being used for cows to walk around. The other 20% makes the pills that cure the cardiovascular diseases from eating the cows. But we've also got a story about a woman fighting hunger, one sandwich at a time.*

While working in a little café, I came to know many of the customers and their orders, most of them got the same thing every day. We always had a line out the door, but you could always count on those faces. One of them was a professor that seemed to live within her own world, walking around like Belle with an open book, though unfortunately, the townsfolk didn't follow her around and sing. I witnessed her walking into walls three or four times, and I only saw her for twenty minutes per day.

She always came in at the same time between classes and ordered the same caprese sandwich with the same Caesar salad. She used to sit at table sometimes, if the restaurant weren't busy. One day she started ordering a second sandwich and leaving immediately afterwards. I figured maybe she had met somebody. I didn't want pry or to interrupt *Moby Dick,* that book is like six-hundred pages.

After a few months of the double order, it became normal. Same time, same order, just doubled. One day I happened to be leaving right after making her order, so I caught up and we agreed to walk to campus together. It was far less awkward then I expected, and it wasn't long before we reached campus.

"What department are you in? I've always wondered what kind of professor you are."

She laughed, "I'm just a teaching assistant. I'm getting my Masters in Linguistics, if I can manage to finish my thesis. After seeing all of the administrative nonsense, I don't think I ever want to be a professor."

"I can only imagine, especially in those classes with hundreds of kids. I had like five TA's in my government class."

"Government, huh? Are you a poli-sci major?"

"It was a minor of mine, until I realized how ridiculous it was. I don't understand why they call it science; it has nothing to do with anything scientific. Everyone just quoted the news from the day before, even in my Philosophy of Gov class. They had no interest in learning much… They seemed to be there to reinforce their own ideals. I was looking to learn about something I couldn't find."

"I totally understand that…I switched majors three times before my junior year…you'll figure it out. I'm sorry but I've got to go, gotta eat this wonderful sandwich you've made me before my next class! I'll see ya tomorrow, it was nice talking to you!"

I said goodbye and watched as she turned around and walked back in the direction we had just come from. What a sweetheart, she had walked with me past her building just to let me finish rambling about my philosophies on government.

I was curious how far she had gone past her destination, so I popped my head around the corner. I was also unaware there was a linguistics department, I wondered where they were hiding. She was sitting at a bench, eating her sandwich with a man dressed in rags. He was eating the second sandwich.

My eyes welled up worse than the end of an episode of *Undercover Boss*. I never charged her for the second sandwich again.

...The Fuck?

Is my burger ready for 23?

Two minutes.

You said that two minutes ago.

"Well, fuck. Fine here you go," I gave it to her just to get her out of my face. I have ten burgers on the grill, amongst twenty other things, and she's asking me about the burger that was ordered six minutes ago.

Let's get tables 24 and 65 out. Got those other tenders? Fries up?

Fries up, tenders in the window. One minute on that shrimp for the salad.

Walking in! 2 kid tenders, 4 fries, 3 orders of wings, all going b-b-q. Just drop a basket of fries. Need a mozzarella stick, too. Grill-Three burgs, 2 medium, 1 medium rare, and a grilled chick- no bun.

Heard, heard, heard.

"Heard," I reply robotically, as I always do- despite the fact that I have my own printer and I have to read the tickets, anyways, he yells every order to me and derails my train of thought. I have night terrors in which I spring up from my pillow and exclaim "Heard!" to my empty bedroom.

With four other employees working three stations and serving fifty customers, I am currently cooking ten burgers with two different buns and three different types of cheese, three grilled chicken sandwiches- all topped differently; two steak and cheese- one without peppers, one without cheese; an order of snow crab, and an order of mac and cheese. While I cook this, I have to listen to multiple employees holler about all of the other things being cooked in the kitchen. Oh, and the waitresses.

Plating two wings now, dropping three. Can I get an all-day?

The guy at 23 said he wanted his burger well-done. Look, it's red in the middle.

"Yet he ate three-quarters of it? You stood in the damn window asking me where it was, so I put it on the fucking bun and gave it to you. I assumed he must be in a rush- it's now been ten minutes since you placed an order for a well-done burger, and you asked me for it after six. It would have been ready right now if you didn't rush me. Now I've gotta cook another one." I knew this would happen when I plated the burger. It happens on a daily basis.

"He asked me if it was ready, I'm sorry. Whatever. He wants a new one," she demanded, dumping the burger and fries in the trash and heading back to the dining room to say, *"We're sorry, there's a new burger on the grill right now. Your meal is on the house tonight. Would you like a beer while you wait for the burger?"*

What a waste of…everything. It's hard not to address the fact that this person ordered a well-done burger. This means they want the limited amount of flavor in this frozen beef to be cooked out of it, so that it may be smothered in cheese and bacon. If you order a well-done burger at a restaurant, the cooks are laughing at you. McDonald's is always down the street, and they have mastered the art of selling well-done burgers.

McDonald's and other fast-food restaurants have also managed to cost the American taxpayers over $7 billion per year because their employees are forced to take advantage of every possible government service. Don't worry, McDonald's is against deforestation in the Amazon, they just announced it to the world. I guess it's easier than apologizing… a commercial pointing out that the number one reason for deforestation is cattle-raising wouldn't sell any beef. It's very simple, even if McDonald's does not get their beef from Amazonian cattle, everyone else in the United States has to because all of the domestic beef is being overcooked, frozen, and served through Mickey D's windows.

It does seem as if people have forgotten that their bodies only require a few things to survive and one of them is food. It's understandable that people have different tastes, but the processed and frozen food has taken this to a whole new level.

My mother never actually delivered me any cute or catchy aphorisms like, "You are what you eat", but myself and every other living person has heard this ubiquitous quip. It's quite sad that most of us wouldn't even be able to pronounce what we are made of, maybe we should have listened to our parents, maybe they should have listened to themselves…

I remember one night as a child, when I had refused to eat the small amount of broccoli on my plate. My father forced me to sit there until I had eaten it, and I saw this as an invitation. After three hours of staring mindlessly at a few pieces of broccoli, I fell asleep with my face upon the plate. *Technically, I won.* I never ate the broccoli and he had tucked me into bed.

"You are what you eat!" was written beneath the government-issued food pyramid in all of my classrooms from which I learned about nutrition. After I had left school, the government realized it was making a terrible suggestion. It's no longer a Food Pyramid and I have no idea how to feed myself. Maybe that's why everyone eats at restaurants so often. They are just *deeply* confused.

This tremendous confusion has led to an American population of which 40% is overweight, and 50% are ingesting at least one pill daily just to function like a human being. Nearly half of all adults in the United States have a self- inflicted disease related to cardiovascular health. 10% of us have diabetes, and a lot more have high blood pressure.

Most of us, including myself, consume several cups of coffee per day, jacking ourselves up with caffeine just to counteract how tired we are from our body trying to digest unnatural lumps in our stomachs.

It's really simple: eat all of the processed, unhealthy food now. Be immediately satisfied, and spend the second half of your life suffering and spending your money trying to fix it before you die. Heart disease is the leading cause of death in the United States, and it is primarily caused by bad dieting.

Maybe we need some catchy phrases and statistics to sway the population toward caring about their own bodies. How about this one: *One quarter of what you eat keeps you alive. The other three-quarters keeps the doctor alive.*

Too long and mathematical. Here's one without fractions, maybe simplicity is the key.

Let food be thy medicine.

Your welcome, government. The cute saying has been around for thousands of years. The guy's name was Hippocrates, most people call him the "Father of Medicine." If you've never heard of him, perhaps you've heard of the Hippocratic oath, the ethical promise a physician makes when entering the medical field. He's kind of a big deal. We've spent a long time trying to complicate things, but **let food be your medicine** is all that needs to be said.

Plaster that everywhere and make people consider it on their own. It will sink in. We don't even need a pie chart, plate, or pyramid. Food is medicine, stop consuming placebos and wonder elixirs that solve nothing.

The food you eat has a direct effect on every part of life and somehow that appreciation was lost. It directly contributes to your body's functionality and appearance; most of us care about at least one of those things. To rush the process of putting food entering your body is foolish. Not to mention, cooking and eating together is a fun experience. Cultures were built around the dinner table, around fires, and at feasts.

Do you know how much more impressive it is to cook for a date, than to take them out and pay for their meal? Oh, how impressive, you've got a job like the rest of the world. Eating in, you will spend half as much. The experience is personal and much more relaxing. *Netflix and Grill, baby.*

Maybe you don't care about the cost. Cooking for someone sure beats rifling off awkward questions while you wait for someone else to bring the food. You can put on some music of your own choosing. Ice broken.

More importantly, if you eat that processed shit from the restaurant you'll be hungry again in an hour because it contains no nutrients. All of the calories, none of the nutritional necessity.

The seafood that you would actually want to eat without frying it or smothering in butter will not be found in a fifty-pound cardboard box that was shipped across the world and tossed in a freezer. Nor will a delicious burger come from a frostbitten tube of congealed cattle muscle that has been frozen for six months and has now been thawing in the sink for an hour. Tasty.

Here's an experience with thawing meat I had at a chain restaurant with many locations nationwide. For the bloggers trying to locate the particular restaurant where this occurred- forget that effort and go to the nearest restaurant. Walk straight into the kitchen and try not to throw up.

Lunch was busy, from start to finish. It had been steady throughout service, enough to keep me working with no chance to compose myself. The dishwasher isn't in yet and the back is full of leaning towers of plates. The sink is full of hot water and soap, overloaded with the customer's dirty dishes.

The soap used in restaurants is almost lethal. The standard process for washing dishes is wash, rinse, sanitize. The plates are washed with soap, rinsed with hot water, then dunked in sanitizer and placed on a rack to dry.

At one small kitchen, we kept the container of sanitizing liquid on a metal sheet tray. It was stored in a corner out of sight, and when spring-cleaning that we noticed the sanitizer had been leaking. The middle of the tray was dissolved, the sanitizing liquid had eaten right through metal. It hardly seemed like that should be anywhere near food, but what do I know? The stuff glows neon red. This chemical dries on almost every restaurant plate nationwide.

As expected, the water is disgusting, and the remnants of wasted food on the plates float to the top. The water is a shade of iridescent reddish-orange-green, some color they would only have a name for in a makeup aisle. At the end of the rush, the dishwasher clocks in and drains the sink.

I had gone through all forty-something burgers prepared for lunch. Midway through service, I had only one burger left prepared. When I see the dishwasher, I ask him to grab some ground beef from the freezer to thaw, because obviously they didn't pull some out for me yesterday.

He grabs a tube of ground beef from the freezer and tosses it in the same sink the dishes were in, despite the fact that he never rinsed the thing. He fills it with water and walks away. It's also the same sink used to thaw the bags of raw chicken which arrived frozen. The amount of blood fills the three-foot-deep sink about halfway. I wasn't watching him; I took for granted that the sink was clean. Turns out, so did the dishwasher.

A lunchtime straggler came in and he ordered that one prepared burger. I made it for him and let out a sigh of relief. "86 burgers for now, I just finished both of those hotel pans. There's some thawing out in the back sink, but it might need a little longer."

At the end of lunch, it seems thawed and ready to go, until I noticed some chunks of things and scummy water that had entered the plastic wrapping.

"Did you clean out the sink before you filled it up again?" I asked the dishwasher.

"I didn't really look at it, I just threw it in there and filled the sink up..."

His voice trailed off with a clear indication that he knew he had fucked up. He's just a sixteen-year-old kid there to wash dishes, he has no responsibility to be aware of food safety. It's likely doesn't know the proper temperature of the refrigerator.

I drain the sink and pick up the beef to discover that at the bottom of the plastic wrapping, there is a dime-sized hole. The leftover dishwater has made its way into the beef tube. Even with no hole, I probably wouldn't have used the beef after being in that water, but I am *positive* most cooks would give it a rinse and make some burgers.

In fact, most managers would consider the wasted food cost before tossing the beef. Surprising, considering restaurants spend billions wasting food in all sorts of ways.

For every person who has ever worked in food service, how many times did the stupid managers ramble on about "food costs"? Most restaurant managers or chefs are actually given a bonus if they are able to keep their spending down on food. I've never seen any of them do so effectively. Restaurants waste 33 billion pounds of food per year.

I toss the dishwater-soggy tube of meat back in the sink to deal with later, and I have gone outside to smoke a cigarette. I may only have two minutes before another order comes.

"Stepping outside for a minute." I grab a plate of extra fries to shove in my face while I have the chance. There are always extra fries.

Any restaurant that sells French fries throws away several trash cans full of them per day. When the place is busy, it is absurd for the cooks to count the orders. In most of these places, the fryolator baskets are continuously filled with fries, over half of which are usually dumped in the trash. That is not an exaggeration.

Ask a waitress or cook about it. The cooks eat them all day long, the waitresses beg for them. They have to bring customer's meals out while they salivate. I've seen a few waitress' eyes well up with tears at the very the sight of a dumped basket of fries. I usually put extra fries in the window for waitresses to eat, because we're all hungry, being around the smell and sight of food all day. Several managers have told me to put excess in the trash, not to give them to the waitresses because of "food cost." It's better they go in the trash.

Fuckin' managers.

It's necessary to walk away for a moment after a lunch rush like that, even if it is a half-assed break. I stand in the back window and look at the order screen, I can hang out here until I see a ticket. If lucky, I'll get five minutes.

When I see an order come in, I open the back door and my fellow cook calls back, "You're good, man, you can chill for a minute. It's just a mozzarella stick, I've got it."

I light up another cigarette because the first one went so fast, it felt like I didn't smoke it. I take my time with this one, granted the freedom to have no concern for orders. I take the time to sit for a nice fifteen minutes, a rare occurrence. In the restaurant industry, you do not get breaks like other jobs.

When I head back inside, I wash my hands and grab a new apron. I head back to the service line and see three tables had placed orders while I was outside, and they've just been sent out. The waitress is passing through the double doors to the dining room with a tray of meals.

I clean the grill and get myself a glass of water, it's finally slowed down, and I can take time to think. I start to stock up my cold ingredients, making my way to the back fridge. As I pass the sink, I notice that beef is no longer there. I don't see it in the trash can and I'm pretty certain I had left it. I figured I'd ask about it, to make sure I'm not losing my mind.

"What did you do with that beef that was in the sink?" I asked the dishwasher.

Before he could reply, a voice came from the grill, "A couple of burgers came in, I had to make them on the fly. That burger was thawed and good to go."

Without a word, I run for the dining room to check if I could just prevent these people from consuming this atrocious meat. It had only been ten minutes, but the customers are sitting before empty plates, calling for the check.

This really happened. Six burgers from that repulsive batch of beef went to the dining room before I could even react to the situation. Three people consumed double cheeseburgers mixed with chicken blood and dirty dishwater, containing a soapy mixture of everything left on previous customer's plates.

It seemed pointless now to tell them what had just happened. I finished out the day and went home. Clearly it tasted fine because the plates are almost empty. I just have to wish them luck and hope they don't die.

To me, this event was completely insignificant, and I've seen lots of things like this happen. Usually unintentional, often resulting from poor communication. That doesn't make it any less disgusting.

After I went home for the day, new ground beef was properly thawed and made into cheeseburgers for dinner service. Business as usual.

Apparently, one of the women who had consumed a cheeseburger at lunch called before dinner asking to speak to a manager. She informed him that she was almost immediately sick after leaving the restaurant. I don't really know what she expected to gain from the call, but she had asked my manager to check the quality of beef being used.

He apologized and ensured her that he would take care of the situation. Rather than risk it, he grabbed all twenty-five pounds worth of freshly prepared burgers and threw them in the trash. Tremendous waste, and nothing was solved.

To avoid diving into another topic that already has hundreds of books about it, I will take a quick sidebar to point out that aside from most kitchen practices being disgusting- this food is really, really bad for you.

Somehow, the illusion that common restaurants are different than Burger King is pervasive in American society. Truthfully, the difference between fast-food and your local wing joint or Texas Roadhouse is miniscule. Their ingredients come from the same places Ask someone who works at a chain restaurant or your local diner.

90% of the restaurants in the United States are serving the cheapest possible ingredients they could use to compose a menu. This is good business, bad culinary practice.

At thirty years old, I often wondered why I was so tired by the afternoon. Why every single day felt like a tremendous chore- no matter what I changed, I was tired by 3:00 pm and my brain was useless. A great night's sleep and a healthy breakfast- it didn't matter. I tried everything, or so I had thought.

When I stopped eating the food from restaurants at which I worked, I was full of energy and lost fifteen pounds faster than I could convince myself to go to the gym. It was hard to do, given that the food was free and available to me, but I realized that things that come cheap or free almost guarantees poor quality- especially regarding food.

The restaurant will fill up again tomorrow, and I'll spend my day serving grilled cheeses to incompetent and lazy people. I should be grateful, they give me a job, right?

The Plastic

This feeling had been away for a long time. An overwhelming sense of purpose delivered by phone in the middle of a Wednesday afternoon. I wonder if I'm looking too much into this, and after publication and few handshakes, most people will just carry on living their lives as they did before. Personally, I can't think of an easier way to solve ten issues at one time with almost no effort.

I had to teach myself to force optimism, particularly when my cynicism affects my life. The privilege lies in choosing to be miserable, though much of my time is spent wondering why others aren't quite as miserable as I am. Don't you see what's going down? Though I suppose the world wouldn't be quite as interesting without that constant resistance.

Relationships were the hardest place to make optimism happen, and each partner came to realize that this sardonic behavior was the core of me, after they had so much time had been spent convincing themselves that I was going to change. Maybe I was misleading. We'd break up, and I'd debate in my mind for a few weeks, maybe telling myself I need to change. A vicious cycle.

I always found myself alone at the end of the day, and comparatively happy about the fact. It was better than the modern version of a relationship. I may be in love with Aubrey Plaza, but I can only watch *Parks and Recreation* so many times while you scroll through Instagram.

I take a seat at the booth and order a coffee, thinking about the possibilities. Even just to move up to a big city paper would be nice. I know I am counting chickens, but as I continued to read the numbers and scroll through pictures- I know I am on to something. It was clear that this had started to be a topic of discussion, already published in *The Atlantic* a few times, more frequently as time passed. A teenaged girl in Sweden quit school and told the world many of the things I am saying, but they seem to have pinched her cheeks and claimed she didn't understand.

The EPA, USDA, FDA and every other abbreviated government service related to food or resources had all published lengthy and informative articles, full of colorful graphs and fantastic pictures of actors recycling. I think the United Nations even said something about food waste, but I don't even really know what their purpose is, so I'll leave them alone.

Had anything changed? Am I wasting my time?

"Simon?"

"Melissa! It's nice to meet you!"

"Same, thank you for meeting with me, I appreciate it."

"Oh, you have no idea. I am so very glad to see you. Please, for the love of god, where did you hear about this? I can't believe this law has been in effect since 1996," I probably could have let her finish sitting down first, but I'm shaking in my seat.

I'm so sorry. I am just so excited. For the past few months, I have been drifting mindlessly through meetings at city hall and reporting on the police chief's drunken behavior, wondering what went wrong with my life. Believing journalism had died- and then there's you."

Her confusion decorated her face. "I'm really not following you… We just need some food at the bank, we're completely out of supplies. I have plenty of money, but I can't keep spending it like this. At this rate, I'll have to go back to work. I'm almost singlehandedly feeding fifty, sometimes seventy-five people on a daily basis, but I can't watch these people suffer."

"This is my point Melissa; we are going to fix a broken system. We are going to shout about it from the rooftops, because this is the most important issue facing humanity right now, and most of them aren't even aware of their participation."

"To get more funding for food banks?"

"Forget the funding my dear. The food bank will benefit, but this is so much bigger than that. The food bank shouldn't even need to receive government money or funding from anyone. The entire food industry is wasting tons of food, and it doesn't have to be wasted. Grocery stores, restaurants, schools, hospitals, people in their own homes. Let me search for it it…. Here we go… 80 billion pounds a year. 219 pounds a person. Per year. Information readily available on the EPA website."

"80 billion pounds of what?"

"Food waste. In landfills. Per year."

"Get the hell out of here… oh jeez, now you've got me swearing. My mother would have washed my mouth out with soap, even at 35 years old. 80 billion pounds? With a "b", billion?"

"Believe it. This is what we're going to fix. Together, we can help redirect all of that wasted stuff. Most people just don't even know what to do, the rest of them hope someone else is taking care of it. You found the right guy for this job. I need a story that actually has some value, that cannot be ignored. This is that story. I feel like I've been working towards this my entire life.

I worked at a country club in college. I used to throw away buffet trays full of food when they had their social mixers on Saturdays. Probably enough food for fifty people. They hardly ever touched it, but each week- the same party. We would spend the entire day preparing food, serve it up in a buffet tray, and then empty at least 75% in the trash at the end of the night. We had to keep the trays full throughout the night to ensure good presentation, and which they could not have cared less about. Only enough to complain if it were empty. I did that once a week for three years. The chef wouldn't even let me take a plate home. Don't even get me started about college.

Melissa, it was wonderful meeting you, but I have some phone calls to make. I apologize, and I assure you I am not usually this frazzled. We begin tomorrow, I will come by the food bank in the morning."

I left the restaurant assured that this was work that needed to be done. The ideas flowed faster than I could record them. One of my first revelations was simple, as I tried to recall my time at that country club and other instances of waste. Just working at that place had opened my eyes to opulence I had never seen, and my first introduction to the mass production of food.

There are many things that working in a restaurant exposes you to, and it becomes impossible not to divulge some of these nuggets of wisdom when eating out with friends. Even just understanding the simple operation of the restaurant can open the eyes of others. Don't order the fish on Monday, there is a reason it's a special. Remember David Koechner in that movie *Waiting*...

Push the fish, it's about to turn.

The writers didn't need to create this line for the script, it came from hearing it in a restaurant. I've heard this so many times, it is hard to count. I've made stews from beef that looked like it was cooked before it went in. It wasn't expired, per se, but I wouldn't want to eat it. I certainly wouldn't want to pay $17.95 for it. That's why the consumer won't know, and I won't be forced to toss out ten pounds of beef. Food cost is important.

Most places will offer that fish for one more day, it's perfectly edible if it's fried. Fish and chip special? You got it. It's likely cod because it is ordinarily cheapest- but overall, it's unlikely you even know which type of fish you're consuming.

Actually, just don't order the special, because it usually exists to dispose of some ingredients that need to be disposed of, and you're the perfect disposal. They'll feed them to you instead, at full price. This is maybe the only way that restaurants spare food waste. It doesn't help much though; the restaurants alone are responsible for 33 billion pounds of the national food waste. A single restaurant can produce 25,000-75,000 pounds of waste in a single year.

About 11 billion pounds of wasted food come from places like schools, hotels, and hospitals. These numbers do not include the amounts of unrecycled plastic from containers, or the amazing amount of fryolator oil disposed of daily.

The USDA estimates that the restaurant industry spends $162 billion per year spent transporting, cooking, and disposing of food that is never eaten. This startling estimate does not include the farming resources used, or money ultimately spent by individuals to counteract their health problems which stemmed from eating out, such as the $500 per month many Americans spend on insulin.

It breaks down to three different types of restaurant food waste, most which never actually breaks down:

Pre-consumer:

-**Giant portion sizes.** Quality over quantity should be the rule. If you are eating a meal that fills a plate the size of a steering wheel, you're eating crap. I'm not suggesting the portions you see in a cooking show on tv, but there is a limit.

-**Spoiled food**, before it is even opened or served, due to transportation or storage. The food provided to restaurants travels more than the average American

-**Scraps,** such as trimmings and bones of meat; unused vegetable parts like skins or celery ends. All of the damn lettuce. You know how you go to the store and buy that bag of spring mix and it just sits there until you toss it out? Imagine that on the scale of a restaurant. In all restaurants, nationwide.

Post- consumer:

Uneaten food left on plates. As mentioned, the portions are often too large, but there is responsibility on the customer. Do you need an appetizer *and* an entrée? You certainly shouldn't have an appetizer at lunch. If you're going to order all of that food, you better shove it in your damn face. Your mother would have made you. If you just can't eat it, bring it home in a cardboard box and feed it to your animal. You just paid too much for this meal, get your money's worth. If you're in a city, take it outside and give it to the first homeless person you trip over.

Overproduction of food to meet customer demand- customers as a cumulative entity are terrible. Last night the restaurant ran out of something, and three people flipped out on the waitress. *Never going back to that place.* To avoid this happening again, the cooks make a double batch. Now they're stuck with it; the restaurant is empty because you went on Yelp and wrote about how the restaurant had terrible service.

Packaging of ingredients. I have thrown at least 5,000 one-gallon plastic mayonnaise jars into trash cans. I am one cook, and I am only thirty years old. That's only mayo. These containers are also used for ranch, blue cheese, and nearly all salad dressings.

Disposables:

Wasteful resources like napkins, straws, to-go containers, paper towels, trash bags, plastic wrap. These are the small items, this waste is multiplied exponentially when considering the packaging involved with transporting mass-produced food.

So much of our food often makes a cross-country tour just to rot in a landfill. The restaurants represent a larger portion of the food wasted, along with grocery stores and farms. At home, we pile on the rest because there is no option available for disposing of food waste. This is not an excuse, just a temporary roadblock.

It's quite a cycle that blinds us to the realities of our extreme demands. On average, U.S. citizens spend 10-15% of their yearly income on food. That is significant, and so is the idea that each of us averages $4000 spent on eating out alone.

I remember leaving a roadside diner years ago, as a gang of four travelled across the country in a forty-foot travel-trailer. It was tiring right from the very beginning, living on the road and being in each other's faces constantly.

We had been on the road for weeks, supplies were slim and our wallets were looking even slimmer. We were searching for ways to pick up some extra cash or get free food from somewhere. It was getting to that point of desperation.

I had just spent my last $300, which we were only able to obtain by returning my brand-new gas-powered generator. We hadn't even used it yet, but by selling it we had committed to candlelight for the next three months.

We kept pushing on and on. In retrospect, we were as dumb as could be but at the time it was as simple as, *we are going to reach the West Coast. We'll find jobs and get more money we arrive. We can make it.*

"Let's get back on the road. Did you leave a tip?"

"Yeah, it's all set," he called back, loading his pocket with napkins and straws from the waitresses' stand by the door.

"What are you grabbing those for? I can understand the napkins, but why do we need all of these straws?"

"Just to have… I don't know," he seemed to be annoyed, like I was ridiculous for wondering why he would just grab a bunch of things he doesn't need.

"Just wasteful, really. When are we gonna use straws? They'll probably just end up in the trash."

"Does it really matter? They're already made and they're here, who cares?"

"Are you serious? You just took half of their straws at that booth. They will have to refill that with straws from the back, and then at the end of the week they will order more straws to replace the box. Keep clearing shelves and they'll keep filling them, because the production doesn't take place after it's been sold."

"Never really thought of it like that."

This seemed like complete idiocy to me, until I realized that without being involved with a process as simple as refilling straws in the dining room, it may actually be hard to visualize the process. Until you've seen a four-foot tall box full of 20,000 plastic straws go empty in less than a week, it may be hard to comprehend.

I suppose this is why environmental activists make nightmare videos of slaughterhouses hoping it will shock its viewer into agreement. Most people don't even want to see it, and sadly, most of us find a way to be convinced that this just cannot be the same meat we're consuming.

There are also terrifying videos of plastic piled as high as skyscrapers and stretching for miles, but they aren't very graphic, and most people don't want to sit down after work and watch a documentary called *Plastic Wars*. Millions of people watched the viral video of the sea turtle with a straw stuck in its nose. They talked about reusing straws for a week or two, then completely forgot. It wasn't *my* straw. *"Oh my, that poor turtle! So glad they saved him. Can I have a large Coke, please?"*

In the 1970's, there were a series of commercials on television, which most Americans over the age of forty will remember. Behold *the wonders of plastic*, they used to say. There were a variety of people using a wide range of products and exclaiming their praise for the many possibilities of plastics.

Some of these commercials feature children proclaiming their love for plastic despite lack of understanding the inherent evil involved with the message. The commercials are so surreal that I was convinced it was a skit from *Saturday Night Live*. Turns out it was just good old propaganda, just like DDT pamphlets.

These ads were paid for by the Council for Solid Waste Solutions, which was formed in response to the revolution occurring within society. All of that Earth Day nonsense. An actual revolution of the mind, in which a society shifted its behavior and began to assume some responsibility.

The first Earth Day in 1970 reverberated quietly through the decade. The plastic industry responded and formed The Council for Solid Waste Solutions, created for the purpose of managing public opinions of plastic. They saw a world shifting away from its products, calling for bans on plastic bags and straws or specific types of plastics like styrofoam. There are thousands of types of plastic, and as one recycling director pointed out, "A milk bottle is as different from a soda bottle, as a piece of paper is from an aluminum can." In addition, there are thousands of different companies making varietal milk jugs.

Most people don't realize why the public chooses to focus on styrofoam. Almost all of the public is aware of chlorofluorocarbons, or CFCs, that used to be inside of aerosol cans. They were banned in 1978 because it is a poisonous gas. Styrofoam is a very thin plastic that is inflated by injecting CFCs, making it one of the worse plastics possible. Somehow, this use of a poisonous chemical was banned in our bathroom sprays but not in the containers which often hold our food.

The Council for Solid Waste Solutions is not a "council" in any sense of the word. The name is dripping in manipulation, conjuring an image of a group of old men in suits discussing important recycling matters. Recycling is their sworn enemy, and the only real solution is for them to stop existing. This is nothing more than a group of Faustian plastic whores who make commercials for abusive pimps.

Council for Solid Waste Solutions has changed, it has a different name now, the North American Man/Boy Love Association. Maybe it was Plastics Industry Association or something. What's the difference? The easy thing to remember is, anything with plastic in it is inherently bad. **Plastic is very, very bad.**

One commercial for plastic actually said, *"Plastic- it picks up where nature left off."*

Excuse me sir, did you say nature "left off"? Where has it gone? The sun rose this morning, and I had to shave before work. I'd be willing to bet it'll happen again tomorrow without plastic.

Seeking accurate information from the Council is impossible, revealing their secrets would cause them to lose their entire industry. They're probably not the type of person you would want at your neighborhood barbeque.

As idiotic as it may seem, plastic bags were actually invented for environmental purposes, to avoid the chopping of trees to make paper bags. The first plastic bags weren't thin and single use because hardly anything was meant to be disposable back before mass-production. Today, plastic bags are banned in some states, and many more are about to vote on doing the same. They are the most visible form of waste, at landfills or just on the street.

The average use of a plastic bag is about twelve minutes, but it takes about five hundred years to break down. This statistic is interesting because we have only been producing them for about one hundred years. Sounds a little dramatic but even if it takes *one year* to break down - that is way longer than the car ride it was used for. The life from your favorite store to your home and into the trash. Then it will sit in a landfill through generations.

We live and we learn, if we're allowed. When a commercial for a product comes on the air, your very first question should be, "What are they trying to hide?" or "Why are their sales so poor that they felt the need to beg for more customers?"

Don't skip that commercial, someone poured their heart and soul into selling you some shit you don't need. How rude of you!

The plastics industry banded together and responded to the Environmental Protection Agency with a public relations campaign which made this substance seem like the most marvelous invention known to man. The truth was quite the opposite, and in many ways, the plastic industry is on the forefront of the war against humanity and the earth it inhabits.

How would most of you feel if a commercial with the Marlboro Man came on the air right now, and bragged of the health benefits of smoking? I hardly think it would air more than once, and whoever was responsible for putting it on the air would be trending and unemployed by the end of the day.

If you would like a modern example of this behavior, ask two friends what their opinion is on high fructose corn syrup. In my own lifetime, I have seen back-to-back commercials providing me with completely contradictory information about this mysterious substance.

It wasn't confusing anymore when I noticed that the commercials praising high fructose corn syrup were paid for by corn farmers. They had formed their own version of the Council for Solid Waste Solutions, to battle the new naysayers. The same exact way plastic makers formed the Council. Someone said, "Hey, this stuff seems bad, let's talk about it."

Corn farmers said, "You better shut your mouth, hippy. My entire life depends on growing corn, and I'll be damned if I lose my family farm." Who could blame them?

Everyone, actually.

The corporations know it, too. I can guarantee they have another public relations campaign ready to go. The Plastics Industry ran another one in the 90s and 2000s, declaring that *Plastics make it possible.* If I have any success, they'll launch another campaign in response to this book. Stay tuned. Everyone fell for their lies more than once before. John Milton wrote a great slogan for the plastics industry, long before they even existed, *"So farewell hope, and with hope farewell fear, Farewell remorse: all good to me is lost."*

Fool me once, shame on you. Fool me twice, shame on me. Can you hear The Main Ingredient coming through the stereo? *...Everybody plays the fool, sometimes. There's no exception to the rule...*

Here I am, fighting the plastics industry before I've finished with the food wasters. One step at a time. I've still got to convince my boss to let me spend the next few months digging through grocery store dumpsters, visiting landfills, and interviewing employees. That is, if he hasn't cleared my desk already. I had almost forgotten about yesterday.

The Starving

"I'm dumbfounded. I don't know whether to write about recycling, food waste, or the secrets of the restaurant industry. You are blowing my mind," I interrupted my new friend. He had been spewing stories from the moment we shook hands. I hardly even had to ask him any questions, he just rambled on.

"Wally didn't even tell me what was really going on here, we met up with Melissa and gave her some food the other night. He started talking about how he didn't feel like being in the newspaper or losing his job, but I don't understand why he would lose either. I'm glad to give you stories all day.

One time, on the first day of a new job cooking breakfast, I was completely overwhelmed by this new kitchen. They showed me around and then left me to my own devices, trying to learn a menu while simultaneously serving it. Trial by fire, as it is in most restaurants. Throw the cook in the mix and see if they can handle the heat. You know the expression.

I was in the weeds, bad. While cooking six separate orders of three pancakes, I had managed to plate the wrong order. A disappointing stack of raw flour and butter on a plate went out to a woman who was an executive in the building. She thanked me and walked away, only for me to realize that she was given uncooked pancakes. I had put them on the grill left to right, got distracted, and took them off the grill in the exact opposite order I had intended. The edges were probably fine, but there's no way she didn't find liquid in the middle. I had just flipped those over.

Twenty minutes later, I see her again, walking straight towards me. I can only assume I am fired, who would employ a cook that can't make a fucking pancake? It's only my first day, maybe I should just run; and they'll forget I ever showed my face.

"Those pancakes were amazing. Was that yogurt in the middle? It was delicious, I hope that becomes a regular special."

"She sounds like an idiot," was all I could think to say.

"Oh, not at all. She was a rocket scientist, and I'm not kidding. She's the head of the department," he pulled out his phone, typed something and handed it over to me. A picture of an actual aerospace engineer, one of whom apparently enjoys raw pancakes as long as she thinks it's yogurt.

He had been revealing stories of kitchen life for over an hour now, and it seemed like he could carry on for the rest of the day. He also possessed one of the most honest and refreshing demeanors I have ever encountered in all of my thousands of interviews. He actually asked himself questions and then answered them. I just saw there in awe.

"Male waiter, huh? You ever realize how funny it is, that old sexist joke about women belonging in the kitchen, making sandwiches? Isn't it funny that, much of the time, restaurants are structured in the opposite way? What are you doing out here, boy? You should be in the kitchen, make me a sandwich!

It's because most restaurants do not involve "cooking" in any real sense of the word. Everything is so backwards that even the sexist stereotypes don't work anymore. What a topsy-turvy world. This ain't your grandmomma's cooking and its ingredients sure as shit don't include love or soul. The menu exists because it allows the cooks to mass produce that particular dish as fast as possible. There may have been a chef involved with its recipe creation, or it may have just been found on the internet. Then the restaurant figured out a way to make that same dish one hundred times a day.

This usually includes methods of preparation like "par-cooking" which involves pre-cooking meats, so that their preparation time is reduced, and it can be served quickly. Your $60 filet mignon probably began its cooking process before dinner service. Ever wonder why there's a 50/50 bet on a piece of grilled chicken that it tastes like rubber? That's because it was cooked halfway hours ago and stored in a pan. It may have even been fully cooked, drained of its moisture completely and reheated for your pleasure.

The vast majority of us cannot afford restaurants that have stars, so this is what we eat. Imagine if your mother said, "We're having dinner at six, and it's almost noon! I've got to cook the chicken now and cool it in the fridge before I reheat it for dinner!"

I had to chime in, it was time to get back to the office and pick up Tom for lunch. It was always easier to get him on board with a story if I get a beer or two in him. "I haven't eaten at a restaurant since I began this project, before I had even heard your stories. I've been throwing my apple cores into the nearby woods because I just can't bear to put it in the trash. Anyways, we're going to pick this up tomorrow because I still haven't convinced my boss to let me write this article. I'll see you in the morning."

I leave the restaurant to have lunch with Tom, and once again, the man is full of surprises. My poor editor has become so conditioned to life as a journalist that he sometimes forgets to think like a person. Just to float the idea of writing about food waste, I pointed out the starving folks that hang out down town as we passed them. The food bank only opens twice a day, but the competition to eat before food is gone forces most of them to set up camp as close as possible.

"…and we're not supposed to say starving anymore, it's food insecure," Tom informed me as I pull into the parking lot of the White City plaza, reluctant new home to the *Daily Mirror*. Last year they had to down size and take a second-floor office because the rent was unaffordable with circulation down 30% in just a year.

"I don't have time for that shit. The word insecure will not be found anywhere in this article. You're making me feel insecure about my choice of employment," I let out, trying to remain composed, "These people are starving. Let's take a stroll down the street and ask a few of them."

There is a significant homeless population in town, and if they're not waiting outside the food bank, they're often found by the old rubber factory. They used to be able to squat inside the building, but someone hired a security guard to protect the defunct and crumbling building.

Citizens that live in the area have tried guerilla tactics to shoo the people away. They have placed boulders on the sidewalk; soaked the area with hoses during winter; scattered bags of playbox sand, amongst other things. They always come back; there really isn't another place they can sleep without being arrested for trespassing.

We decided to take a walk down there before heading back into the office. He was convinced that I was just going to do yet another piece on the town's homeless population. I will wait to drop the real bomb. *I need six months to visit grocery stores, restaurants, farms, and landfills; you're going to pay me for it.* Real research, old school journalism.

The two of us walked in silence for the first half of the trip, until I felt a responsibility to apologize to the guy who had my back for years. "I just want to say sorry for the other day, and I appreciate you running the article."

"I owed it to you. Plus, it got some recognition on social media and the website traffic has been higher than ever in the past few days. It won't get us subscribers, but we may just show up on a few Google searches now."

"*Journalist tells off the industry*. I don't know if that's what I would call it, but some of the responses were fun to read. I've got an even better story," I attempted to draw away from the other day immediately.

This visit to the homeless would make his eyes peek open, then I'll come in with eyelid speculum. I quickly discovered that Tom is still the man I admired before his Editor position squashed his ambition. I didn't hesitate to put him right on the spot.

Approaching the factory, we find a man lying prostrate on the ground, staring at the sky.

"Let's ask this man right here. Hey man, you hungry?"

"Starving, dude."

I laughed hysterically. It may have been the most disrespectful thing I have ever done. I could have spent the entire day pedantically arguing with Tom, but this man had just taken care of that in a matter of seconds.

"I am so sorry, that is not funny at all," I must have been brick-red in the face, but I was still smiling because the man's answer could not have been more perfect. I had to ask him one more question. "Well, Tom, how about that. You can feel good about calling him starving. He has self-identified. Can I ask you another question sir?"

"Fire away, boss."

"How would it make you feel to know that the government now uses the term "food insecure" rather than starving?"

"Same way it felt when I was shell-shocked after Iraq, and they told me I had post-traumatic-stress-disorder. Buncha talk to keep the regular Joe from understanding. I just wanted some pills to forget the sight of dead eyeballs lookin' at me."

Tom had seen the light, and it was a swift, visible change. He gave the man a hug and handed him the last two twenties in his wallet, telling him, "Thank you very much, my friend. Lunch is on me. Have a good day, good luck out there, brother. We're down at the *Daily Mirror*, feel free to come by for coffee or lunch whenever you want."

It's easy to tell how uncomfortable a person is in a given situation, just by counting how many ridiculous nicknames they give the other person; like those people that call children "slugger" and ask them if they "like school."

I knew this would be sufficient to ask Tom for the time I needed to gather my story. I pulled up all of the websites- EPA, USDA, NRDC and showed him all of the colorful charts. I showed him the EPA's backhanded attempt to reduce food waste by 2030 and the Good Samaritan Food Donation Law. I even offered to cover the obituaries whenever I could.

"I can promise you; this is the biggest story on the planet right now. The discussions pop up every couple of years and nothing happens. We can make a difference. Isn't that why we got into this business?"

When we returned to the office, he went straight to the computer and typed "Arnold Abbott" in the search bar. "Read this," he asserted, and began to walk away.

"I was just like you, not long ago. Actually, I tried to write about a very similar topic. My boss gave me one article, and it was basically a summary of Reuters' article. Unfortunately, this is just the man's obituary."

Arnold Abbott, lifelong activist who fought to feed the homeless, dies at 94

By LISA J. HURIASH

SOUTH FLORIDA SUN SENTINEL |

FEB 22, 2019 AT 6:05 PM

Arnold Abbott, the soft-spoken lifelong activist, has died — five years after he drew international attention for feeding the homeless despite threats he'd be jailed.

Abbott, of Fort Lauderdale, died Friday at age 94, according to his family and his attorney.

Abbott began feeding the homeless on Fort Lauderdale's beach in 1991, although it was illegal to provide such a social service on the beach. Years later, the city demanded that he stop, but he refused, saying he and his corps of volunteers had a right to feed the homeless so they could eat on the beach like anyone else.

"I've been fighting injustice all my life," Abbott told the South Florida Sun Sentinel in 1999 after a show down with police. "I was always taught I am my brother's keeper. I'm a fighter."

His defiance put the city of Fort Lauderdale in a pickle because it wouldn't look good to actually follow through on its threats. "I don't want to prosecute him," the city's prosecutor said in 1999. "He wanted to be carted off and be a martyr. We're not going to do it."

I stopped reading there, it was quite enough to set me off. I guess I hadn't even read the part that mentions he was a fucking World War 2 veteran. Even if you're a hardcore pacifist, you can empathize with that war. This man wasn't drafted or something, he fought in the last war that seemed to have any basis for fighting. *War! What is it good for?*

Well, this crazy bastard with half a mustache seems to think that we're all pretty worthless and he's rounding up people and killing them. Apparently, he is gaining quite a following, and he just started invaded all of the surrounding countries...

I think even *Edwin Starr* would have at least advocated a strongly worded argument. War certainly is good for absolutely nothing, but damn, we should check out what's crackin' over there.

I had heard of this veteran and his story; it was all over the news. I didn't even connect the dots when I had discovered the Food Donation Law. The police were illegally persecuting a wonderful man by citing fabricated local laws that contradicted a three-year-old federal statute. They were all fired, right? I can't seem to find that story.

I have to incorporate Arnold Abbott into this story somehow.

I can't even believe that any human being would object to someone giving away food. That is certifiably insane. Benito Mussolini would have been proud. That lovable leader would have also loved the term "food insecure."

The invention of this term is nothing more than a sugar-coating to hide the forty million people in the United States that are currently starving. Their kids go to school with your kids. The family in the apartment next door, or in the house across the street may be starving right now. Many of them have a job and a place to live but are unable to afford food for their family.

For the average person who consumes an American dinner on a daily basis, you can't even fathom the idea of splitting a McDouble and small fry between three children and calling it dinner. I would order three McDubs for myself if I were stoned.

You probably can't imagine the feeling of not knowing if another meal will come tomorrow. *That's fucking starving.*

I've personally described myself as starving, and I'll bet you have, too. I went grocery shopping two days ago and my mother just casually told me she was starving as she looked through our loaded refrigerator. Twenty minutes later, after the family takes turns looking, we've determined it's all the same shit we ate yesterday and order a pizza. Hooray, convenience.

There are so many homeless in the United States that somebody actually walks around and counts them like livestock. Sure, some of them may have made poor life decisions that led to them being there, but most of them are symptoms of a broken system.

Did I say homeless? I meant Home Insecure. *They're, like, so insecure about themselves.* You should see these characters, just a bunch of nervous nellies second guessing themselves, worried what everyone else thinks.

They are symptoms of a broken system which, rather than repair itself, changes names like ExxonMobil's oil ships. Everyone has their own experiences, but I can safely assume most of us immediately picture a starving person when the word is used. Even if you aren't one of us regular folk that encounters homeless people daily, you surely watch television. I can envision the protruding ribs of children, and I feel Alyssa Milano staring me right in the eyes now.

The word starving immediately draws forth the image of people who need help, and we can't be using a word like that in political conversations. Let's call them insecure. We're well on our way to Lois Lowry's nightmare vision of language precision.

If you asked one of the 40 million starving or 600,000 homeless in the United how they felt, I'd bet my life that not a single one of them would say insecure. Disappointed, cold, hot, uncomfortable, angry, sad, starving, tired, homicidal, suicidal, thirsty, even just downright bored, would be the most popular answers. Somebody should ask them, next time they throw the lasso and round 'em up for a headcount.

For three hours I was in a daze, reading of Arnold Abbott and similar stories and eventually finding my way back to food waste, which brings me back to landfills, then recycling, then plastic, then the oceans. I can hear Fleetwood Mac singing, *"You would never break the chain…"*

Damn the dark and damn the light. This stuff is depressing, and I feel like I'm in the *Twilight Zone.* Every book has the same company names, whether it's about plastic, environment, or waste. Dow Chemical, Dupont, Monsanto, ExxonMobil, BASF, the names appear over and over again. The number of articles, documentaries, books, and YouTube videos gives the impression that everyone is aware.

The government, the newspapers, even the bloggers aren't talking about it enough. It's been sporadically discussed in all sorts of media outlets but no change has come. *National Geographic, Rolling Stone,* and *The Atlantic* seemed to have published an article every four years on these environmental topics, in addition to many, many documentaries.

In 1963, President John F. Kennedy gave a speech informing the American people, *"If we do what is right, now in 1963…"* They never got around to doing what was right.

We haven't even started, and it's been sixty years. Every president since JFK has given a public service announcement in which they declare environmental crisis. Regardless of which American king you think is best, they all had something to say about it.

John F. Kennedy warned that the population would be more than double by the year 2000, and he was right. He was concerned we would run out of land. Considering the Superfunds and shipping trash all over the world, I think we're getting pretty close.

Lyndon Johnson must have hired an English major to write his speech. He told Americans, *We need to stop poisoning our air, or we become a nation in gas masks groping our way through these dying cities and the wilderness of ghost towns that the people have evacuated.*

Richard Nixon delivered the "Question of the 70s" in front of a gigantic American flag, asking us if we will surrender to our surroundings or make reparations for the damage we have done to our air, to our land, and to our water.

Gerald Ford talked about renewable energy, solar panels and such. Did people like him the most, or was solar power just the easiest thing to try? Key word there is *try*, we're still pretty bad at utilizing solar power. Keep looking up. The ocean could *never* generate any power.

Jimmy Carter told Americans, "If we don't act soon, we will face an economic, social, and political crisis that will threaten our free institutions." It seems he was right.

Someone told Ronald Reagan to talk about endangered species and the wilderness, I'm assuming it was the hot topic that month. Maybe that was when everyone started sadistically joking that polar bears are turning brown? Though honestly, browning would be far better than drowning.

Big George Bush had the audacity to quote a Native American proverb, *"We don't inherit the Earth from our ancestors, we borrow it from our children."* The video of him reading this line is quite entertaining. You can tell he hasn't read it before that moment, and he smiles as if to say, "Damn, that's beautiful. Mind blown." In case you're not aware, the Bush family owns an oil company. He still gave a speech acknowledging that we were fucking up the world. That's something.

Bill Clinton had Al Gore with him in office, so he had to hear about the environment all of the time. He practically screamed at America about emissions and greenhouse gases, warning of deadly heat waves and droughts, flooded coastal areas, and economic crisis. We're currently experiencing every single one of those symptoms, and the fun has just begun.

Maybe he wasn't screaming, and that's just how Clinton always addressed the nation, but I'm too young to remember any other speeches he gave, except that one about the blowjob, he was very calm then.

Little George Bush gave a speech focusing on clean air with a generic statement promising to address climate change. Oil money paid for his caviar and he still publicly acknowledged environmental issues were out of control.

Barack Obama said we should cut U.S. emissions by 26% by the year 2020. I guess we forgot. For all of you that are missing him, make him proud. For those of you that hate him, do it to spite him because it didn't happen while he was there. *Thanks, Obama.*

Oh, well. The presidents probably didn't write those speeches. Turns out we could begin to solve all of those problems with food waste, though. The easiest battle to start. It would have the same effect as taking millions of cars off of the road.

The food waste generates about 20% of the methane, or "greenhouse" gas produced in landfills. We could solve the clean air and emissions goals right there. Lots of types of food can also be turned into forms of energy, so even Gerald Ford could rest easy.

Jimmy Carter's crises would be addressed as we save money, create new jobs, and push the government to do what they promised for the past sixty years.

We can make those reparations for the Dick. We can finally "do what is right" as we were asked by JFK back in 1963. We can begin to address problems causing economic, social, and political crises. It doesn't matter which of these characters you pledge your affiliation to, they've all asked us to control yourselves and we haven't listened. They didn't help, but let's not point fingers.

Scream out your favorite catchphrase, whatever helps you get on board.

YES WE CAN… MAKE AMERICA GREAT AGAIN

Oh, I went there, and it almost rhymes.

Two political slogans of equally despised presidents who seem to be unconditionally loved by two "opposing" groups of people. Anyways, to those of us who can't take it seriously, they are all the same. They're all equally terrible to me, but that's not important. Democrat, Republican- whatever helps you sleep at night. I'm a Hufflepuff man, myself. I just really like the name.

I've put the cute catchphrases together for you. We'll all pretend both of them aren't stupid and maybe we can call ourselves *The United States*. Catchy, right?

I'm sitting here slowly dying inside as I plow through statistic after statistic about environmental issues. Minding my own damn business conducting internet searches and stumbling upon random chains of information that never seem to end. *No way, Del the Funky Homosapien is Ice Cube's cousin! How did I not know this?*

How did I end up on the Wikipedia page titled *Category: Rappers from Oakland, California?* I've got to get to the topic at hand. Grab a cup of coffee and get back to the grind.

I log into Facebook, to quickly digest the headlines that I will pursue through more legitimate sources. At the top of My Feed, it says, "Visit our Climate Science Information Center!"

Uhm, okay Suckerburg. Thanks for incorporating my Google searches into my Facebook page… Might as well see what it's all about. The following is from Facebook's *Climate Science Information Center*:

Climate Change by the Numbers

---Humans have caused about 1.0°C (1.8°F) of global warming since pre-industrial levels, according to scientific estimates.

---At the current rate, global warming is likely to increase to 1.5°C (2.7°F) between 2030 and 2052.

---Limiting warming to 1.5°C (2.7°F) isn't impossible; but would require unprecedented transitions in all aspects of society.

If that doesn't light a fire under your ass, what will? Thanks for trying to change the world, Facebook, valiant effort. Now they can say, "We have written and published statistics, worked with scientists around the entire globe to closely monitor the effects of human beings on the environment. We are dedicated to promoting change."

Nestle's website says, *"Dedicated to Maine"* or *"Dedicated to Michigan"* and we all know what that means. DowDupont is *"Dedicated to Sustainability"*. Maybe we should all be frightened of "dedication."

There are many other things I could criticize, right? At least Facebook tried?

I don't think so, there seems to be no *real* effort there. The page is bland offers one statistic that most people don't understand. That is public relations, an attempt to make it look like they tried. Do not be fooled. We need legitimate help. Facebook wants to get involved with the elections, but the planet isn't sending any checks. Just oxygen, food, water…

Any other piece of information about climate change would have been better. Maybe even the fact that a temperature increase of 2 degrees at the equator is an almost 12 degrees increase at the poles. You know, the location of those melting ice caps that everyone seems to worry about.

How in the world does Facebook's page help anyone understand anything? Did a person even write this, or was it generated by an algorithm? How do I go about managing the temperature of the Earth's climate? Should I carry bags of ice around and scatter them on the street? *"Huh, just two degrees? Maybe it ain't so bad? Forget these reusable shopping bags, I can't even remember to bring them half of the time!"*

This is actually a serious matter, to raise the temperature of the Earth by two degrees. Most people wouldn't think that. Relative to most of our lives, two degrees is intangible. If I adjusted my thermostat by two degrees, I don't think I would notice.

After exiting Facebook's "Climate Change Information Center" I can't even find it again. I've typed it in Facebook's search bar and still found no results. I wonder if anyone else had ever seen this page, not that it would matter. This is part of the problem. Even the President of the United States is capable of spewing off some shit about saving the trees and the polar bears.

When I attended Monsanto-Coca-Cola-UMass-Amherst, they gave *themselves* an award for sustainability and hung banners about it around the campus. I debated transferring schools.

The town of Amherst does not pick up trash like most towns, despite inviting 30,000 students into town for nine months of the year. There are six or more other colleges in the area, too. Students are expected to dispose of their trash on their own or pay Waste Management. I don't know a single college student with extra money to spend on trash disposal. They can hardly afford to buy food to throw away. Most students find dumpsters, I was always able to use the dumpster of the restaurant I worked at, and plenty of other students used it, too.

Hey, Netflix, or any of you streaming places trying to take them down; want a free lead? Head to a college town during the last week of the school year. Tens of thousands of kids move back home, and most of their furniture is dispensable. Televisions, couches, beds, everything that must be removed from within their rental is forced outside with no destination. It's pandemonium.

I've witnessed two dudes hurling an unwanted couch from the back of a moving Dodge Ram; fights over dumpster space, an entire living room of furniture left arranged in an empty parking lot, and so much more. There is quite a bit going on, it's actually exciting. I was always ready to redecorate. My apartment during senior year actually allowed me to see the dumpster from my window, I would watch race to grab things before the person threw it in.

I never paid for a piece of furniture in college, which included a 42" TV that was left on an abandoned couch. A graduate of the university actually runs a profitable business collecting and reselling the furniture. Colleges and universities, just like the rest of the nation, are not held accountable for their trash. They are profiting from the people that produce the trash, inviting them to live there, and ignoring the symptoms.

This is only one particular example, of one type of institution. As of now, only individuals are being held accountable, and we're not doing a very good job. I am guilty. When Best Buy tried to charge $50 to dispose of my television, I threw it in the dumpster at a T.G.I. Friday's. I am a jerk for doing this but I didn't even have enough to buy a new TV, forget giving the store more money for a broken one.

We aren't facing the threat of the Second World War's limited resources, but we will be soon. We can easily avoid it with a little control now.

The Grocery Store

I had more than enough to show the public how wasteful and useless the restaurant industry can be, but with no access to grocery stores, I was only able to peek into dumpsters at night. They were always locked. Over the course of a weekend, I had visited forty-three grocery stores in the area and only two were unlocked.

In those two dumpsters my expectations were met. I had found a treasure trove of food that had no explanation for being in the garbage. Half of the dumpster was fresh produce, most of which looked completely edible. I climbed right in and the first thing I noticed was the crunch of celery and lettuce. I wiped an orange on my shirt, unpeeled it, and gave it a try. It was juicier than the oranges I had purchased last week for full price. I paid $4 for six oranges and they were wrapped in plastic. Somebody should let them know that oranges have their own natural casing.

There were endless amounts of pre-bagged salads in all sorts of varieties, atop a refrigerator-sized piled of yogurt, all of which had a "sell-by" date that wouldn't happen for three days. Not to mention, it would be delicious for far longer than that.

If there is no mold or funky odor, you can generally eat it. You do not need to be a chef to judge the quality of food in your refrigerator. There is absolutely no standard on these dates, most of them are nothing more than a guess regarding quality. The government has declined to pass the *Food Freshness Disclosure Act* several times, which would make the dates have standards. A few companies have even been called out for intentionally putting early expiry dates, as a subtle way of pushing sales.

I found probably fifty cartons of eggs buried beneath the produce, which revealed a whole area of plastic-wrapped sliced mushrooms, all of which appeared to be fine and had two more days on the provided date.

Potatoes, corn, fifteen gallons of almond milk, a few jugs of orange juice. It was quite a few shopping carts full. I hadn't even dug very deep yet and I estimated $300 worth of groceries were visible in the top layer.

The lower portion was like an entire bakery had been condemned in the middle of the day. Enough products to fill a bakery with ease. To make it worse, almost all of it was wrapped in plastic. I counted at least fifty loaves of French bread, there were cakes, muffins, bagels, cupcakes, and cookies of every variety imaginable. All of them had a sticker which said, "Oops, we made too much! Reduced price."

If I owned this grocery store, I would fire the baker. I'm sorry to let you go but you baked enough bread to fill the bottom three feet of a 20-foot dumpster. It really doesn't matter how inexpensive it is to bake bread, that's just silly.

In 2008, Stop & Shop grocery stores realized they were wasting a lot of money and resources on unsold food. They began to collect data and worked to stock their displays more effectively. They still have *Super Stop & Shops*, but they made more effort than most grocery stores. It benefited them greatly. In a single year, they were able to save $100 million nationwide. By simply tracking sales, they were able to stock effectively and provide the same service without wasting so much food or money. Too bad that's only about four-hundred of the nearly 40,000 grocery stores in the United States.

For some reason, I found about twenty bags of frozen blueberries that probably never expire, but even if they did, the date on the bag was three years away. It seems like terrible business practice to throw anything of value into the trash. I could understand if there was a meaningless date on the bag and it had passed, but as far as the store is concerned, they just threw money away. There isn't a single industry other than food that wastes its product so willingly. I haven't done the research but I don't think Wal-Mart just tosses last year's HDTVs into the dumpster. I'm positive they don't throw new models in there.

Wal-Mart is a terrible perpetrator of food waste, and having taken over as the number one supplier of grocery products nationwide, they have a responsibility to help fix this immediately. It won't even cost them a cent and they'll look like wonderful angels. There are almost 5,000 Wal-Marts in the United States. This position of power allows them to set an example for the rest of the industry. Right now, there is a beggar in front of a Wal-Mart while an employee is throwing fresh food into a dumpster out back.

It's happening at grocery stores across the country; and to hide this, they purchase locks for their dumpsters, or spend $20,000 for a trash compactor. A grocery store shouldn't even need a dumpster, they are selling fresh food. Aside from the cardboard used to ship products to them, and some scraps from the prepared foods department, what in the world would they need to be throwing away?

I wanted to hear some of the excuses straight from the managers, and I tried to convince Melissa to wear a small camera but she refused. It probably wasn't necessary but I felt like I was watching her turn into Nellie Bly right before my eyes. This is a much safer mission, but the spirit remains.

Melissa had stories to tell, but her old grocery position as manager never forced her to directly face much of the problem. She was actually quite excited to go *undercover*. Her hopes for a big case were squashed when the food began to flow. She had been back to every place she had visited, and provided a copy of the Good Samaritan law. It wasn't long until the food bank was loaded with food, so much that she was seeking other food banks to take some of the donations.

Most of them were shocked and more than happy to begin donating, now knowing there were no ramifications. A few managers still refused to believe even though the statute is published on all of the government websites. I guess even the ".gov" websites are hard to believe these days. I can sympathize, I heard they used to recommend DDT for polio prevention.

I began spending more time with Melissa, helping at the food bank occasionally. It was strange to see that most of the products were packaged and "expired" but looked perfectly fine. Many things appeared to be in the trash simply because the date was unreadable, even though it meant nothing to start. We had enough hummus to last for years. The expiration dates were set only ten days from the meaningless sell-by date, but the store decided to stock an entire refrigerator for display.

Wouldn't it be far more economical to try and sell these products for half-price? Even just sell them for one dollar, and at least something came from it. Otherwise, the grocery store paid to stock the product, then paid for disposal. It would even be more economical to give them to all of the employees or hand them out to customers at the checkout. *Happy Wednesday, sir, you're the fourteenth customer, here's some free hummus. Come see us again soon!*

At home, you can freeze almost anything and extend its refrigerated life. It's always better when food is fresh, but even hummus can be frozen. If you can't finish it and it is getting to be that questionable time, freeze it before it goes bad. Organic shoppers often find freeze-by dates on their products, because that stuff is expensive.

Many of the problems in grocery stores can be resolved at our homes. Our shopping tendencies force waste inside of the stores, and then we waste much of the food that we purchase. The waste at home is almost twice the amount wasted at the grocery store, it just seems less because it is distributed amongst all of our trash. Then it's hidden from us at a landfill.

The Landfill

The three of us had decided that we were going to take a trip to a landfill and get a real idea of the problem we were facing. It seemed like the final step after collecting experiences and data related to grocery stores and restaurants. The farmer's problems would be resolved through these efforts, and there was no need to address them yet. I assume most of them are completely fine with saving all of that time and money. There won't be some whacky battle of organic vs. non organic any longer, because a cow eating fruits and vegetables is as organic as we can get. It also makes a much better steak, better burger, better tacos.

I picked the two of them up just before a round of garbage trucks was scheduled to make its way to the dump. Seeing the landfills in their tremendous size is a lot like new parents at the hospital, looking down at a cute newborn baby wrapped in its little blanket.

Oh, my goodness, I just want to eat you up.

I should have eaten you up is more suitable for witnessing these landfills, but the song remains the same, it bears a familiar feeling.

The point being, the sight of it takes your emotions for an abrupt chaotic rollercoaster that overwhelms the brain and causes us to say things cannibalistic or generally creepy things like, I just want to squeeze your little cheeks!

Can you believe we made that? How on Earth did this wondrous thing come from us?

Whether it's a tremendous pile of garbage or a newborn human baby, the loss for words has a similar feeling. The two should be acquainted, they'll be sharing the Earth after you're gone. We're producing both of them at exponential rates, faster than any point in human history.

In Los Angeles county, Puente Hills holds the honor being the largest landfill in the United States, at a whopping 500 feet high and stretching 700 acres. For reference, that's about the height of the Great Pyramid in Giza and an American football field is 1.32 acres. The California dump is closed now, and no longer accepts garbage. It is now a tumor on the Earth. Maybe that's better than the ocean for now, but all of that buried plastic will ensure the surrounding land and water are forever tainted.

New York knows all about this, previously holding the honor for largest landfill. Since the 1970s, Fresh Kills Landfill accepted 28,000 tons of garbage per day. It is now being converted into a park, and in fifteen years nobody will know it is sitting atop decades of trash. In fifty years though, everyone will know exactly what lies beneath. In seventy-five years, we may have the first *X-Men.*

Supposedly, the name Fresh Kills comes from a misspoken Dutch word, *kille,* which means stream or riverbed. A perfect mistake, considering the place smelled like death and violated so many laws that New York and New Jersey held celebrations on the day it was closed forever.

When it closed, the trash began to make international journeys. In 1987, there was a famous barge of trash stuck at sea, unable to find a place to dump New York's waste. It sailed a few hundred miles to dump; but residents of North Carolina saw it trying to dock and flipped out. They sent it back to sea with no destination, forcing New York to frantically call other states and countries, all of whom rejected the garbage. They ultimately had to return home to burn and bury it in Brooklyn.

NYC never actually found a new place for its trash, and much of it is actually sent to Virginia, Ohio, Pennsylvania, and Iowa. Beautiful places full of farmland, responsible for a good amount of U.S. food production. America's fucking Heartland.

Fresh Kills was a coastal marsh before it became a landfill. All of the vegetation died off, and it was quickly replaced by rats, gulls, and packs of feral dogs. During 1997, the landfill caused a disaster known as the "syringe tide", when medical waste washed up on New Jersey's shores for an entire year. NYC paid New Jersey $1 million for the cleanup and washed their hands clean.

There are massive accumulations of garbage in the ocean in areas known as gyres. They collect debris that floats from the land and trap it in a circular current, eventually spinning it out to sea. In the United States, the gyre in the Pacific Ocean is so large they gave it a name. *The Pacific Garbage Patch.* This is only one of five gyres, and it may be the worst because it collects the oceanic garbage from the United States *and* China. Most ships have no reason to sail anywhere near the others, so they are lesser known, but no less powerful. There are five Garbage Patches, flowing strong and growing every day.

Most importantly, this is not a continental *patch*. The plastic is broken into tiny fragments that would require microscopic mesh to scoop out. Pictures from above make it seem like a floating mass, but when a ship sees it from the ocean, most of it is tiny pieces floating below the surface. Different types of plastic have different buoyancies and many plastics don't float at all. Scientists believe there is thirty times more plastic on the ocean floor than on the surface, at least fourteen million tons.

The whales that eat plastic bags are extreme examples, most of them are full of plastic fragments we can't see. They are at the top of the oceanic food chain, and almost every creature in the sea consumes tiny amounts of plastic all of the time. Particular fish and many oysters tested in California have shown high levels of plastic in their stomachs. We don't eat fish stomachs, but those oysters are almost made of plastic. *Viagra oysters.*

We can't fix what we have done but we can avoid making it worse. Ocean plastic can't be cleaned. Even if every ship in the world decided to go collect plastic from the sea right now, it would hardly make a difference. We just need to stop overwhelming landfills and forcing our bad land habits into the water. We can't fix the past and we need to stop talking about the future. There is plenty to be done right now.

We need to stop having babies, or stop being so careless and wasteful. The two cannot continue to be cast upon the Earth and left to their own devices. We all had to read the *Lord of the Flies* in middle school; and if you've never driven through New Jersey, you're lucky. Even with the windows up, the odor of garbage incinerators permeates the car.

If you ever wondered why New Jersey smells that way, it's because they are one of the few places that burns **over half of their waste.** Incineration is a poor solution to waste management. The fumes are toxic and the stuff does not disappear. The ash is *still* buried in a landfill.

The landfills always come back to haunt us. Each is only used for a designated period of time, and they are often converted and sold as if it weren't sitting atop twenty years of trash.

In Niagara Falls, New York during the 40s, Hooker Chemical Company was running out of places to store their toxic waste. They convinced the town to hand over control of their landfill, then buried their poisons twenty-five feet down. They covered it up and planted grass. Flowers began to grow.

During April 1952, the company's President hoped that selling the land could alleviate them from future liabilities for the buried chemicals. They sold it to the Niagara Falls School District for one dollar, as long as they agreed not to hold the company responsible for future problems. Inflation isn't *that* crazy, in the 1950s, land could not be purchased for one dollar. This was a sketchy deal. Families moved into the neighborhood and they built schools. Supposedly, the following was written in a letter from Hooker Chemical's lawyers to the company president:

"The more we thought about it, the more interested Wilcox and I became in the proposition, and finally came to the conclusion that the Love Canal property is rapidly becoming a liability because of housing projects in the near vicinity of our property. A school, however, could be built in the center unfilled section (with chemicals underground). We became convinced that it would be a wise move to turn this property over to the schools provided we could not be held responsible for future claims or damages resulting from underground storage of chemicals."

The New York State Health Commissioner said it was a "national symbol of a failure to exercise concern for future generations." He was quite right, it must have been shocking when children came home from the playground with chemical burns, but absolutely nothing changed.

New York is the home to over eight million people and visited by sixty-five million more per year, it's one of the most disturbing places in the world. For starters, when their subway cars are deemed unusable, they put them on a shipping barge and dump them in the middle of the ocean. They claim the deoxidation of metal improves ecosystems for ocean life.

The government in New York have been dumping trash directly in the ocean and shipping it to other states for years. They just slashed the sanitation budget in NYC by $106 million and there are now trash bags piling up in the streets. Maybe it's better that way, it won't end up in some state that's actually worth loving.

Stop visiting New York City, until they can clean up. Open a magazine and you can see the same advertisements. Times Square only looks cool on television. It's full of fast food and 20,000 other clowns trying to take the same picture. NYC is the only tourist destination that I would adamantly suggest a traveler avoid. It may have been cool once, but it's not anymore.

It's the only place in the world that looks better in a picture than in person. There is trash all over the ground and cars beeping all day long. It's the city that never sleeps because there's too much waste and too many people that just won't shut the fuck up. It's just a landfill that isn't full yet because they built all those stupid penis replicas too high. They will just build New, New York City on top of it and avoid the mutants. *Good news, everyone!*

I grew up with the NY rivalry, chanting "Yankees Suck" at Patriots' games; but it has never rung so true. New York is a vile place but it would be impossible to avoid that. The amount of people that swarm in for a selfie and a slice of pie is unsustainable- too many people live there to begin with, and most days, 300,000 people swing through for a visit. Oh, and almost 300,000 more come into the city for work.

The city is left with the trash of that additional surplus of people. They want the tourism, of course, it generates lots of money and provides many jobs. I don't think they want it this way. Maybe they do, but the rest of the world cannot deal with their waste. I'll bet those folks in Iowa have no idea that the nearby landfill is extra waste storage for the Big Apple Core.

New York is a very strong example of a problem occurring across the country. The people of Maine are currently battling to keep Massachusetts from exporting their trash north. Landfills are reaching their peak, and over the past twenty years, most of the landfills in existence have closed. States are paying each other to bury garbage.

In Massachusetts, my hometown built a baseball field and two soccer fields on top of a landfill. It makes perfect sense; the town is full of trash. It's amazing that we cheer our children on as they run back and forth across our childhood garbage. Even better, the landfill ends five feet from a lake, the only fishing spot in town.

On the other side of the state is the city of Lynn. The North Shore of Massachusetts, where people actually have that Boston accent everyone tries to imitate on television. *Lynn, Lynn, city of sin. Ya won't come out the way ya went in.*

Lynn is not far from Salem, where the famous witch trials took place. Ten years ago, Salem built a school called Witchcraft Heights, on top of an arsenic dump, which was temporarily closed and required $16 million to "clean up." It's still open today.

Many of my extended family members have lived on the North Shore for over fifty years. Some of them attended Lynn Classical High School in the seventies. Before their children would attend, the town made the decision to build a new school in a different location.

In 1999, the geniuses making decisions on behalf of Lynn decided it would be a swell idea to build a new high school on their fully-loaded landfill. The town spent $40 million and constructed what might be considered a nice-looking hunk of cement, if you're into bland American architecture.

It took a few years, but eventually everyone complained of the smell; it was unavoidable and nauseating. In the halls, the floors were like walking on a waterbed, tiles bending with each step, causing the students to sink. In the worst places, a sludgy liquid rose up from the ground.

By a 5-2 vote in 2001, the Lynn School Committee formerly voted to accept the new Classical building, a requirement to start the state reimbursement.

"We were told that things were going along fine, and that the building was just settling," recalled Loretta Cuffe O'Donnell, who was then the committee's vice chairwoman. She voted with the majority to accept the school.

Seven years later, while my cousins attended the new *Lynn Classical High*, the school was closed. It had been built atop a landfill, who woulda thunk it'd smell like garbage.

Turned out, the entire school was sinking into the dump. The town spent another $14 million to fix the abomination. They sued the construction company and alleviated some costs, but I doubt the location was chosen by the construction company.

The school is still there, but I'm not sure how bad it smells.

The folks in Lynn are surely used to it, by now.

Standing in the middle of one of these disgusting heaps of unearthly material is something we should all try once. Landfill is hardly an appropriate word, they are mountainous. If Fresh Kills in NYC had been open another year, it would have been the tallest mountain on the East coast. It will soon be a park that makes Central Park seem small, hiding a ticking toxic bomb beneath.

To see a landfill is like the overview effect of an astronaut who sees the Earth from space for the first time. Words are meaningless, just look at it. Unfortunately, looking closer- the Blue Marble has quite uneven edges.

At least seventy million tons of plastic ends up in landfills every year. When you arrive at a landfill, it's the first thing that sticks out. Assorted colors of such a wide variety of plastic products, squashed, torn, mangled. Plastic bags float by like tumbleweeds. It is easy to see why people have tried to ban them.

Isn't it a bit strange that almost every single thing in our existence is made of plastic, and yet the "environmental groups" are always pushing to ban plastic bags and straws- the two **smallest possible items** we could ban?

Many people are unaware of the real nature of a landfill, which is key to understanding the problems here. Landfills function in various stages, and for many of us, the way they operate prevents us from seeing reality. In California, the landfill at which I dumped trash was a mountain that could have easily been used for skiing in a cold climate. The size was unfathomable.

After paying a fee and entering the gate, we would begin a climb that lasted about five minutes. A professional could probably BASE jump from the top. It is hard to process the notion that the mountain below is actually just trash that has been buried. The roads are smooth dirt and all of the ugliness is hidden away from the consumer. At the end, you can see the small area where things are currently being dumped, and it hardly seems like the place has any garbage.

All of this trash is heaped into the ground, and underneath is a plastic liner like you may have in your swimming pool. This is intended to prevent the disgusting sludge that leaks out from entering the surrounding land, as it has in many places, destroying things or causing health problems. In the history of landfills, there has not been one that has effectively contained the sludge, which they call *leachate,* because it leaches and transports hazardous chemicals. This is that brown sludge that would leak from a trash bag with a hole. Picture the amount of liquid scum generated by all of our trash put together, left out in the rain.

Spread around the plastic is a brown, amorphous blob of food waste. Banana peels sit with McDonald's toys, next to pairs of shoes and Subway wrappers. Black trash bags decorate the place, helping ensure that the food in there doesn't decompose. There's a microwave and a couch right in the middle of it all.

Think of the absurdity of sending a bag of *leaves* to the dump inside of a plastic trash bag. What are we preserving them for? Just push them off to the side of your yard and go watch the game. Landscaping is a waste of energy. Let it grow. You worked enough this week.

I've ripped open three trash bags to find nothing but leaves and sticks. I spread them about the landfill, but I hardly think I have saved the planet. The rest of the bags just reek like food that has been deprived of oxygen.

If separated, the food might break down in a pretty short amount of time, relatively speaking. I think they call it composting. By being buried under the conglomeration of stuff, food is cut off from oxygen and unable to decompose properly. Burying it actually causes it to undergo a process called *anaerobic digestion* and produce those greenhouse gases we always hear about. They can be used for energy, if this process is performed in a closed environment. There are a few facilities in the United States, but not many. Most of the food is buried in landfills with plastic, spewing these gasses into the air.

It is a large-scale example of discovering an uneaten sandwich rotting inside of a plastic bag. Open that bag up and the rancid fumes may gag you. It would not be so wretched if it were just sitting on the ground unwrapped. The United States is concealing a few billion sandwiches in bags all over the country, like a bunch of kindergartners that never empty their backpack. Mother Government is working two jobs and she doesn't have time to check in on us.

The garbage trucks run continuously throughout the day. I had scheduled our trip to the dump with the intent to investigate a fresh load. I wanted to see the food before it turned brown with just enough decomposition to manufacture some wholesome methane.

With the frequency of trucks, I was hardly able to get a look at anything. I'd start poking through a pile and two minutes later they're honking at me because I'm in the way. At least thirty trucks had just dumped in the last hour.

I realized this was a fruitless effort and decided to stick to the wealth of information already published on the landfill subject. Almost 300 million tons of garbage produced in the United States, and the largest portion of anything in there is food. If you research the topic, it makes it seem as if everyone were already aware but each year the problem gets worse.

I had enough material to write a book, but the most I could do was publish in the *Daily Mirror* and hope that it was shared on the internet. I spent more time editing than I had actually writing the material. I had to force myself to stop researching anymore because I found myself adding more and more statistics, sucking the meaning from the story. The statistics provide the proof, but most of the time, they don't force the proper reaction.

The Story

It was time for the story to be published, and I faced ten different people from seven different departments suggesting that various parts needed changes in order to avoid conflict. They all came forth with my favorite passages, the ones that took it too far. For the first time, I know what someone means when they say they are offended.

"You can't say they're "raping the Earth." References to rape generally dissuade 40% of readers from recommending. We're trying to sell books here."

They tried to make it seem as if, by mentioning this planetary rape, I was advocating non-consensual sex amongst human beings. My inability to respond made them think I was a horrible person. *L'étranger.*

"The legal department says you technically can't say that plastic is not recyclable, because some of it can be recycled one time. Can you rephrase it to be a little more precise? Do you have some more statistics? I know it will eventually be in a landfill, but can we work around that phrasing?"

I responded to nothing. I tried not to take it personally, but they were trying to remove the heart of the message. More importantly, they were talking about the very parts that would spark conversations.

"I heard that Chevron has figured out a way to make plastic recyclable. Did you hear there is an enzyme that can break down plastic?"

She must have only read the headline, because that "enzyme" requires specific temperatures over 150 degrees Fahrenheit and takes months to break down a single plastic bottle. I could really care less what Chevron has to say, there's no way it is anything legitimate. After checking, their supposed solution to recycling won't be ready for at least ten years. Until then, they plan to keep producing at the same rate. During the time I've spent writing this book, they have overtaken ExxonMobil as supreme petroleum overlords. It hardly makes a difference; they are both remnants of Standard Oil, owned by the same people.

The statistics are boring but the most important factor is humanity. No one wants to be told they need to behave differently. I cannot stand being told what to do, but there are times we all need a little direction. We need some sort of connection.

I learned this fact through standard Americana, playing baseball as a child. Over twenty-five years later, I can still remember the first time I was made to understand what it means to "keep your eye on the ball." Even a person unfamiliar with baseball can understand the expression, and every batter knows this is rule number one at the plate.

It is easily said, though a bit harder in practice. Many children struggle to grasp the concept of watching the ball leave the pitcher's hand and make contact with the bat. It actually irritated me to hear my coaches shout, "Keep your eye on the ball!"

Shut the fuck up, I thought I did. In the summer before Little League, I had a coach that watched me consistently pull my head, taking my eyes off of the ball. He repeated the same thing over and over and I can't blame him. It sounds like a really simple concept, just watch the damn ball. He never got through to me.

One day after a terrible game, the stands cleared and everyone had left. My father kept me at the field. He must have seen *Star Wars* recently because was acting very much like Yoda. He began to pitch to me, watching me commit the same batting errors. Without saying anything at all, he took the bat from my hands and pushed me back to the plate. He walked back to the pitcher's mound, held the ball out and said, "Keep your eye on the ball."

I stood at the plate empty-handed, watched the ball leave his hand and past my body. He continued throwing pitches as I stood watching each ball hit the backstop. After about twenty balls, he told me to pick up the bat. I was pretty good in Little League.

Reduce, reuse, recycle. Reduce, reuse, recycle. Reduce, reuse, recycle. Reduce, reuse, recycle. Reduce, reuse, recycle. Turn it, leave it, stop, format it. Reduce, reuse, recycle. Reduce, reuse, recycle. Reduce, reuse, recycle. Reduce, reuse, recycle. Reduce, reuse, recycle. Reduce, reuse, recycle.

Are you reducing, reusing, and recycling yet? Keep your eye on the ball. Now forget the third part, it's not real. The new three R's are Reduce, Reuse, REGULATE.

Rolling Stone wrote an article six months ago about the lies about recycling and plastic. Supposedly they reach 700,000 readers, I can't seem to find any of them. It blew my mind that the cover didn't say "PLASTIC CAN'T BE RECYCLED". The following paragraph doesn't appear until six paragraphs in, after an ad telling me to "not to back down from ankylosing spondylitis":

"Plastics are just a way of making things out of fossil fuels," says Jim Puckett, executive director of the Basel Action Network. BAN is devoted to enforcement of the Basel Convention, an international treaty that blocks the developed world from dumping hazardous wastes on the developing world, and was recently expanded, effective next year, to include plastics. For Americans who religiously sort their recycling, it's upsetting to hear about plastic being lumped in with toxic waste. But the poisonous parallel is apt. When it comes to plastic, recycling is a misnomer. **"They really sold people on the idea that plastics can be recycled because there's a fraction of them that are," says Puckett. "It's fraudulent. When you drill down into plastics recycling, you realize it's a myth."**

We are surrounded by recycling bins perpetuating the idea that their waste is being handled. I figured maybe some personal experiences would help people see the problem, but it also creates personal attacks that distract from the argument.

It was nice to see new cooking shows and videos taking over the airwaves. As celebrities began to lead the trend, everyone hopped on. Who wouldn't love to have Will Ferrell teach them how to make a nice stir-fry?

Some things were changing, and it seemed like local news stations had aired something on the landfill topic at least once. It was a bit strange watching the ripple effect work backwards. Everyone was made aware but the effects were hardly felt in daily life. Shelves are still filled with plastic items, and based upon the level of production that was taking place before all of this, there is enough for ten more years.

It hardly seemed productive to take things from the shelves, we had to allow time for adjustment. To abruptly change the lives of so many people is nearly impossible without the fear of a crisis of some kind. It was hard to communicate the crisis when it continued to surround us, from our cars down to our toothbrushes. We had given in to plastic, allowing it to infiltrate every aspect of our lives.

There was a time before this demon. It would be quite sad for humanity to capitulate to a chemical. Everything was better before plastic, but many of us are hardly even aware of this reality. We never had the chance to operate without it.

Many people chose to quote various selections and try to guide my words in ways I could never imagine. I saw a trending tweet that said I wanted to end recycling, another said I wanted a complete ban on plastic. A complete ban on plastic would turn the place into Amish country, nobody is asking for that. Just regulation, maybe even some innovation. Henry Ford made plastics from soybeans, hemp, flax, and wheat over 100 years ago. He was forced to stop producing cars when WWII broke out, soon after which he died, and nobody bothered to pursue it again. The amount of technological progress since his time should allow us to be a little smarter with our production.

When you are inside of a system, it's hard to see how it's all hitched together. Once people began cooking for themselves a bit more, restaurants were wasting less. Grocery stores were hardly wasting at all. The stuff that was filling their dumpsters had disappeared. Congress have been discussing an entirely new SNAP system with stores that specifically aim to deter food waste and provide healthy food for families that really need it. The rich folks like the decreased funding going to food stamps. Everybody wins.

It was relieving to see the overnight change in grocery stores and restaurants. They couldn't help the plastic situation much, aside from ordering less items contained in plastic. Most of them are chains though, they don't get to decide what goes on the shelves. The plastic industry would like the public to believe that our food will not stay fresh without plastic. The truth is that if your food is in plastic, it was mass-produced. There would be no reason to wrap it in plastic otherwise. There are so many other options for containing and transporting food.

Dunkin' Donuts gave up their plastic cups, and as one of the larger suppliers of single-serve coffee, that will have huge effect. There are so many alternatives, and many of us were irresponsibly tossing a plastic cup or two per day. The company thought their cups were being recycled, and we really can't blame them. Most of us were living under the same impression.

The food waste, however, was almost resolved overnight by these entities properly disposing of their garbage. Every one of them was already aware of their problematic waste, but they were never given a solution to their problem. As they began to hand over the things they weren't selling, food banks weren't required to beg anymore. I even saw an article from one major city that claimed the homeless population had decreased by 30%, but I knew this wasn't a because they all moved into apartments. It was quite simply because they weren't visible on the street begging for food anymore. Either way, it seemed to please the rich and the poor simultaneously.

The best part was that much of the wasted food began to go straight from farm to food bank. The farmers were living on the "damaged" fruits and veggies themselves, but could never finish the amount that usually goes to landfill. The grocery stores are still hesitant to place the previously rejected items on a shelf, but it hardly seemed to matter any longer. There is now a place for the stuff to go.

Grocery stores are finding little use for their dumpsters, quickly realizing how much food was being wasted. Many of them realized that it was silly to have a dumpster at a grocery store. There's no reason for that much waste to be created in a place selling the fresh and raw food.

When the government finally passed the Food Freshness Disclosure Act, everyone responded positively. Most people had thought there were food freshness laws already. No more wondering if something is legitimate, no more confusing a *sell-by* date with a -*use-by* date or any other useless information. Sell-by dates were incorporated into scanning systems, hidden from the consumer. Likewise, one simple date for all basic products was established by the Food and Drug Administration. Most people were shocked to learn that their food actually lasts much longer.

The stock exchange has seen a new market develop from nowhere. Companies responsible for engineering machines to separate food waste were making millions, supplying the power to farms across the nation. Many regions pitched together to provide a central location where food waste could be dumped, made into compost, and resupplied to farmers for fractions of their former fertilizer prices.

The bills for trash pick-up decreased and many garbage trucks found themselves returning back to headquarters with a near empty truck. Tesla designed an eco-friendly garbage truck that also collects food waste, and it's hard to find a town in America that hasn't picked up a few of these. There have already been a few thousand jobs created, and there are probably 100,000 more on the way. A brand-new industry that had previously existed as a shell is now booming.

It was easy to find the money for its beginnings, once it was realized that subsidies were being misappropriated. Once the money was redirected from soda, grain for cows, and ineffective methods of waste, the industry paid for its own birth. They are even discussing a new Superfund for plastic, though I haven't heard back on those meetings. Nestle doesn't seem to want to pay, but it hardly seems they'll have much choice.

They gave me some regional journalism award, again, and supposedly it trended on Twitter for two hours. After discovering that I had become nothing more than another whiny voice in a screaming sea of meaninglessness, I figured I would make my acceptance speech go viral. The event sold less than one hundred tickets, but they were all in media and they all have phones. May as well go out in a blaze of glory.

<u>The Speech</u>

Thank you for this recognition, it's been an honor. An ego-stroking, empty form of honor, but I appreciate it all the same. I can only hope to live long enough to see the change. *"Of all the words of mice and men, the saddest are "It might have been."*

These times are calling for social recognition. A bit of empathy, a bit of understanding that perhaps we've been doing things wrong for a while. Basic recycling is a great example. The disposable culture hasn't always existed. Before things were produced at such a scale, reusing and recycling weren't just trendy words. They were hardly even words, people just did it. It was economical and it made little sense to dispose of something which could continue to function.

If it ain't broke, don't fix it. If it is broke, fucking fix it.

Remember that scene at the end of *Fun with Dick and Jane* when Jim Carrey tells the public that Alec Baldwin has returned all of the money he stole, and Baldwin can't do anything about it because the camera is broadcasting him live?

All of you plastic makers and food wasters are in the spotlight. You have been called out by name. Try and tell the public you're going to continue what you've been doing; it will make for some great television.

I have seen change that has directly resulted from my work on this project. I have spoken to countless individuals that made it clear they were unaware of the damage being caused and immediately changed their ways. Even if it's buying the cardboard milk container over the plastic jug, it helps. I have visited restaurant owners, some of which were involved in my research, though they were not aware at the time. They have apologized to me as if I am the leader of this movement somehow. I'm nothing more than a distraction from the issue. I wish I did not have to write this book.

The following are headlines from only within the past year:

"Is Plastic Recycling a Lie?" – NPR

"How Big Oil and Big Soda kept a global environmental calamity a secret for decades" - Rolling Stone

"America's Plastic Hour is Upon Us" – The Atlantic

"Big Oil Is in Trouble. Its Plan: Flood Africa With Plastic." – New York Times

"Americans Eat and Inhale Over 70,000 Plastic Particles Each Year According to a New Analysis" – Time Magazine

"We Made Plastic. We Depend On It. Now We're Drowning In It" – National Geographic

This is not an optional issue, and if I may be so very pedantic, it's not an "issue" in the modern sense of the word. It is not attached to a political party, a creed, belief, region, or any possible form of characterization or division we human beings have devised. We're not going to be discussing the political party's "stance" on the matter. You're with the rest of the human beings on this planet, or you're in the way. Wasting resources, wasting life.

Ask your friends, ask yourself, "Have I even wondered how long a piece of plastic would last?" Most people seem to have never considered the question. We've been led to believe that our blue bins justify the use of unnecessary plastic.

If you are a human being living on Earth and you consume food, this is your problem. If you do not need to consume food, please seek medical attention.

My wife said you wouldn't laugh at that one. She's always right, of course…

Ah, there is the laughter. An old trick my dad used every day. His jokes never got a laugh- but it was always resolved with a joke at his expense. Everybody loves a little self-deprecation. Bonus points for throwing in "the wife". If I were married, she may have been right. Double bonus points for the proverbial father wisdom.

I don't care if you "believe" in climate change, though it doesn't make sense. Quite frankly, I could not care less what you decide to eat. I'm not even suggesting changing your mind on anything, it just seems to me that nobody really knows where all of the waste is going, and this is a problem. To look closer and realize that most of the waste doesn't need to be there, well, that makes it feel like we're kicking ourselves in the head, pushing it under the Earthly rug.

Responsibility for your own actions is something simple but has become increasingly complex in this modern age. Imagine, for a moment, how it was before all of these grocery stores and superstores. Imagine your water comes from a well, which you share with the rest of your neighbors. It's about a half-mile up the road, not too bad, but definitely something that makes you roll your eyes and say, "Ughhh, fine, I'll go get it."

You strut back with two big buckets, enough to cook dinner and have a shower. Would you waste a drop? Even the two cows out back drink rainwater because fresh water for the cows would mean six or seven more daily trips to the well. Plus, if each family that uses the well began to make multiple trips per day, the thing will dry out before long.

It's hard to fathom something like this. I buy a thirty pack of water bottles packaged nicely for individual transport. I throw the bottle in the recycle bin and I feel no guilt for that. I trust that my local recycling plant will handle this accordingly. There's a little arrow logo on the bottom, that means my hands are clean.
I think we've realized by now; those recycling arrows lead right up your ass. *The revolution will not be televised* for many reasons. One of them is that the same company owns the media, the farm, and the water company. That doesn't stop the revolution.

Now, I've rambled on and more than half of you lost interest. Here are the things that every human being needs to do, beginning right now, without question. We have persecuted people for less, and those who are wasteful and destructive are worthy of persecution. If the government won't pass the necessary laws, we need to act on our own. The world happens far, far beyond the spectrum of the clowns that represent us.

There is no out of sight, out of mind. You are simply procrastinating. This land will be nothing more than landfills and graveyards for your children. I have no kids, I have no real concern for society's future, but there seems to be a whole lot of you investing a bunch of time into these little creatures. Then your plan is to leave them with your garbage? Again, I'm not parent, but caring about the child is like, priority number one, right?

The cynical laugh at that one. There is still a lot of silence. Do you feel guilty yet? It's okay because sometimes guilt is exactly what's needed for motivation. It gets me to the gym once a year.

If it is sitting together in your trash, it will rot together in a landfill. Does a banana peel seem like it belongs with the wrapper from your popsicle? Will that instant rice bag help decompose the celery ends?

Let's work our way up the chain. All solutions are pretty simple, and it begins with the individual. Johnny Appleseed once said, "Be the change you want to see in the world."

I want to say first of all that I have often heard transportation used as the excuse for lack of food donation. I can assure you, there are lots of people willing to lend a hand, and the internet allows these possibilities to become reality. I have sold a guitar on Facebook Marketplace in less than an hour. One time, I paid a man to drive to Auto Zone, purchase a car part, and drop it off to me in the middle of the desert. I gave him $10, and he was happy for the chance to pick up a few extra dollars. A business or restaurant could easily make a post, "We have trays of food leftover from today's banquet, anyone looking for some free food or willing to drop it at the food bank, come on down! We're open until nine." The food would be gone in no time. Most of us working-class heroes would probably jump at that opportunity right now. A grocery store could do the exact same, if no employee were able to make the delivery.

Individuals and families, there is one simple rule which applies to nearly everything in your fridge. If it smells fine, it probably is fine. Aside from infant formula, there is absolutely no meaning behind any date on a container. Some dates are there because the company felt compelled to guess, but they weren't required to do that. Some companies put it there to force it to be sold or consumed quickly and increase sales. Others put it there for decoration. Until the *Food Disclosure Act* is passed, you can safely assume that the dates on your containers have no meaning.

If you do buy too much, or cook too much, send it **anywhere** but the garbage can. Pets, hungry neighbors, whatever. Compost and start a little garden. There are so many possibilities.

One company helping to solve grocery store waste is called Misfits Market. Their website allows you to make a weekly selection of "unsellable" products collected from grocery stores. Totally random collections of things that can inspire all sorts of dishes. New items become available every week. Cuts out some shopping too. Hopefully soon, they won't be required to travel so far for deliveries.

Stop eating out so much, learn to cook, it isn't that hard, and it can be an enjoyable experience for the family. It should be considered a crime to feed your child fast-food. Okay, sorry. Don't ask for people to make laws and ban things. That's quite un-American, probably harmful to freedom in general. Let's at least make it taboo. You're slowly torturing a child.

Slow down, sit around a dinner table with a proudly prepared meal. Make your child peel the potatoes. Remember when there were chores? It wasn't entirely because the parents were lazy. It was educational.

It used to be a matter of family importance to maintain recipes and pass them down. Maybe put down the black mirror and try looking each other in the eyes, it might make your day a little better. There are so many creative ways to create family involvement in the kitchen. How many times have you heard someone wish for something their mother always made for them, from their grandmother's recipe? Was I the only person paying attention during *Ratatouille?* Ever heard a specific memory about eating a Sweet Onion Chicken Teriyaki? I doubt it. If you have, damn, that's fucking sad.

Don't fret for the restaurants, or the waitresses and cooks losing their jobs. Most of them fucking hate it anyways. There is about to be plenty of job opportunities in cleaning up the destruction of plastic and "recycling", and farming that will offer more rewarding career paths. Cleaning up garbage is no worse than cooking and serving garbage.

Choose your products more carefully. Pay attention to packaging, and I would not recommend eating or drinking food from anything made of plastic. No one actually knows the harm that can be caused yet. Don't let your child be the one they feature on *Today*. They may even end up on *Maury*, "My mom fed me dinner on plastic plates for eighteen years, now I've got a limp and it burns when I pee!"

Mass production and plasticization of everything from food to toothbrushes, clothes, furniture has turned our homes to junk. There was a little more appreciation for the dresser made by your grandfather than the $20 piece of garbage from the shelf at Wal-Mart. They still made you assemble it, too. Just with shitty plastic parts. They have five hundred of them just because know that you'll be back for a new one in a year when that "great value" expires. Nearly all products made of plastic suck, especially if there is *any* other material it can be made of.

If you can't find your way from plastic with particular items, such as toothpaste, toothbrushes, food packages, tupperware, etc. There are actually ways for them to be recycled. It requires a little effort, but it won't even cost you anything. Maybe a few minutes. For example, you can recycle all of the aforementioned plastic products through *Terracycle*. They partner with businesses like Colgate or Rubbermaid and make sure that these products are actually recycled. Most of us throw the toothpaste tube directly in the bathroom trash. It may seem small, but every person in the country is doing the same exact thing. Terracycle takes all kinds of products, and they pay for you to ship the items. They even collect cigarette butts. True American heroes. They can help us to finish out this Plastic Era of American society.

I understand that it's hard to even find some products that aren't made of plastic. Things will change. I know we still need to brush our teeth, and so on. However, I do believe that we are smart enough to find ways to do things without plastic. Human beings seem pretty smart, generally speaking. *Any intelligent fool can make things bigger, more complex, and more violent. It takes a touch of genius — and a lot of courage to move in the opposite direction.*

Watch a YouTube video and learn how to build a dresser with your kid. I'll bet they give it to their child. You won't see that Ikea furniture being lovingly passed down through generations. If someone can learn to speak a foreign language or play guitar on the internet, you can surely screw some wood together.

We have at least 150 years-worth of work to do, to compensate for the past seventy-five. If everyone joins in, we can cut that time down. **<u>How awesome would it be to be the first generation in the history of humankind to have a positive effect on the planet?</u>** That is the epitome of awesome.

Drink tap water. You pay for the water, whether you drink it or not. If you are worried, get yourself a filter and one of those sweet $20 steel water bottles that keeps it cold all day long. You can also buy more elaborate filters for the home's intake or add a pitcher to your fridge for more filtration. There's no excuse to buy bottled water anymore, unless you're in a desperate situation like Hinkley, California or Flint, Michigan. You will now be considered a jerk.

Society, make sure these jerks are exposed. The non-smokers managed to ostracize those cancer-sucking clowns and force them outside. We can do the same to plastic users. A cigarette is nothing compared to a plastic bottle, in terms of waste or pollution. Make the guy with the plastic bottle sit outside. Treat him like a litterbug. Fuck him, and any other plastic people. *Don't buy that bottle of Aquafina, you jackass. I won't be subjected to your second-hand stupidity and support of the devil.*

Learn how to cook, we can all learn together. The inability to feed ourselves is perhaps one of the most pathetic elements of modern humanity. It is very easy. You will be healthier and live longer. You will save money. What else needs to be said? You will be a better at sex.

Kids, when your shopping with your parents at the grocery store, watch what they buy. Don't let them buy plastic, because you will have to clean it in twenty years. Did mommy just throw away a whole bag of lettuce, and now she's buying a new one? Ask her about it. See a milk jug in the trash can? Ask your dad why he doesn't love you.

Tell your parents to teach you how to cook. Maybe you can learn together. It's silly to be an adult that can't cook their own food.

Let's evolve. We should soon be able to say, "Wow, is that *plastic?* I haven't seen that stuff in years! Where did you get it? Do you remember when they made shitty disposable furniture and cars out of that?"

Stores in control of your own inventory; don't sell the toxic shit. Once the plastic water is out of the stores people will quickly realize they have the same stuff at home. They may miss it temporarily but that won't last. I guarantee this. Coke and Pepsi will have glass bottles back on the shelves soon.

Order products contained in things other than plastic. There are always alternatives. It won't take long for most companies to transition from plastic, once they learn that it's poisonous and may be contaminating the food or drink they so proudly produced. **Food and drink companies** already know there are a lot of alternatives to plastic.

Wal-Mart, Costco, BJ's, help us out here. Keep the bottled water off your shelves. I know much of the sales are done in bulk, but the products do not all need to be processed and wrapped in plastic. You could dramatically expand your clientele. You're allowed to control a massive portion of the grocery market. Be a leader. All contracts with plastic users are void, now that we know there's rape and murder involved. If you refused to carry a product, the market would be forced to change. You do realize you have the real control, right? The middle man has the real power. Both the producers and the consumers depend on you making the connection.

Local governments with town trash pickup; select a place in town to compost and start collecting food waste. Promote recycling until we've finished with the plastic. You can do this by picking up trash less frequently than recycling. Many towns pick up trash weekly and recycle bi-weekly. Most towns in the United States have tiny blue bins for recycling, and trash cans for trash. This should be reversed, or at least made to be equal in size.

It will take a little while to get all of the plastic off of the streets, so we have to finish the plastic "recycling" fad strong. We never really recycled anything for fifty years, it's time to give it a try.

Ban plastic products like bottles, utensils, bags, cups, straws, and styrofoam. Anything disposable; absolutely useless products that already have alternatives. It's very simple, and many towns have had no problem making these plastic regulations happen quickly.

I don't know what happened to permit local government to displace the responsibility of waste to companies like Waste Management, but this situation needs to be reeled in immediately. They are not providing the right services and they are making lots of money fooling you, destroying your towns.

Colleges and universities, you collect the money of tens of thousands of students and invite them to live in your town, you are responsible for their trash. Most of them are just figuring out how to do laundry. If you're going to resist, at least educate them about waste.

All schools should compost and educate students about composting. It's a necessity in the modern world. We need to stop forcing natural things to undergo unnatural processes. We needed to stop yesterday, but we'll settle for today.

Students, make your school ban plastic. It's easy to make these types of movements on campus. Stand in solidarity and force your school to recognize your pleas. It's a little crazy to build your future while simultaneously destroying it.

If your school says it has a contract with Pepsi or Coca-Cola, you'll just have to be creative. There has to be a legal basis to nullify a contract, considering these companies have lied about recycling and they're killing the planet.

College campuses have plenty of space for compost, and more than enough money to properly handle waste. If you are in college, pay attention to your waste and hold your school accountable. Your voices are often heard the loudest.

All Schools, stop carrying plastic. Let the vending machines empty until we find a new solution. Otherwise, you may as well give each child a cigarette and tell them about Santa.

There needs to be bins for food waste available for the children, and they should be educated on plastic. They should know that recycling is the DDT or Watergate of our generation. It may be another ten years before the government reacts. *Knowledge is power.*

The kids should also probably learn how to cook, considering it's one of the few skills we actually need to stay alive. It is just as important as every other subject in school. Anyone who disagrees, I will gladly argue that point live on national television.

Restaurants, if you can make it through this and there is a reason for your existence, like a unique menu, fresh local ingredients, or something otherwise amazing; then good for you. Glad you could make it. In order to continue operating, restaurants should take these simple steps, to avoid being such a detriment to America.

Separate your food scraps; donate unused food; form recipes around utilizing all ingredients. Stews and soups are a fantastic way to use "ugly" produce or scraps from onions, celery, peppers, and other vegetables. You can make broths and reductions that add extra flavor to almost anything.

You can expand your menu with the useable ingredients usually thrown in the trash. Appease the older crowds that seem to eat soup year-round. Make something weird with tomato ends for the vegans. Just search the internet, it is full of recipes.

Stop cooking more than is necessary, even if you have to make the fries appear red on the ticket or learn how to better estimate the fry count. Don't fill the fridge with prep if nobody came in last week. Don't order more of something if you don't need it right now. Don't drop two baskets of fries when it's dying down.

If you misjudged the prep, give it to an employee. Even a customer. You can wait until they have eaten and paid if you want. See if they know someone to give the food to, or stop by somewhere yourself. You probably drive by plenty of starving folks on the way home from work.

If you do follow these steps, your food cost will go down, the bill with the trash company will decrease, and they'll be less trash to take out.

A lot of restaurants are going to go out of business but that's just got to happen. There is no need for 650,000 restaurants in this country. I'm sorry, restaurants, but most of you have manipulated us for a long time. Some of you deserve sympathy for pouring your heart and soul into these businesses. That does not change the fact that we need most of you to stop operating.

It probably should have happened when the food became 90% processed, anyhow. You served us what you could afford, now we're going to push our own microwave buttons. You have to admit, it's pretty fucked up to serve pre-packaged vegetables and meat you didn't have to cut, trim, or prepare. You're just an extra step between me and my frozen processed food. What's your purpose, really?

Grocery stores can easily stop selling products in plastic by purchasing other brands. Accept everything from the farms which sell to you and donate "ugly" produce or anything otherwise deemed unsellable. Of course, we are not talking about donating spoiled milk or some expired fish- but an apple with a bruise? A broken head of lettuce? A sandwich left on the prepared food display? If that amount donation is just insurmountable, you can dedicate a reduced-price shelf for those on a budget, or those who don't mind and simply understand that the food was grown in the ground, transported in a truck, and then thrown into a refrigerator. You would be bruised, too.

Don't overstock or overorder. Shrinking display cases will help dramatically. There are many ways to use the space that don't include overstocking. If you are consistently tossing something from the same display because it doesn't sell, find a way to arrange it better. Don't keep filling the space if it will never empty. Use some of the unnecessary space to try and sell damaged goods that may have otherwise been wasted. Cut the price in half and someone will buy it. Donate ANYTHING that won't be sold.

Farms, give the grocery stores the stuff that you are currently deeming unworthy of sale. They used to reject it, but now they're all going to realize that we can deal with a bruise on the apple. In fact, it would help so many of us be able to afford healthy food.

Allow *gleaning*. This is when you allow volunteers and hungry folks to come in after harvest, clean up after you and scoop the unharvested food. Across the country, the unharvested food is over ten million tons. You don't work hard every day for that. Gleaning has been a practice for thousands of years; it was actually the law in particular societies. If you read the Bible, it's even mentioned in there. There is no down side. Less clean up, and all of that exhausting work won't be for nothing. Everyone needs a hand sometimes.

National Resources Defense Council, thank you for your efforts. We're still dying out here. How is Nestle even a company anymore? Can we start some sort of app to connect food-wasters with food-needers? Technology can be used for some pretty sweet purposes.

I am not an advocate of any government program of any kind but I understand how difficult it is to do everything on your own. That being said, why isn't the NRDC an official part of the government? At least imitate the institution, why wouldn't a nation have a department specific to preserving its resources? Shouldn't we measure Gross Domestic Waste? It has quite an impact on Gross Domestic Profit.

Citizens must demand that the Federal Government pass the Food Freshness Disclosure Act. It has been voted on repeatedly since 2001. This act would force a standard on the use-by, sell-by, freeze-by dates that currently mean absolutely nothing. What exactly does the Food and Drug Administration do? They aren't administrating control of the food in the only way they possibly could.

Dear Lords and Ladies of America, how is privatization of water legal in a country that celebrates freedom? Why did we allow these corporations to destroy our country? In order to keep giving you our money, we will need food and water. Your serfs humbly ask for your help. President, Governors, Senators, Congress, Supreme Court, Mayors, Town Councils, all of you politicians. If you are on board from the get-go, you will win the affection of many. You may even get your name in a history book, it's kind of hard to do these days. If you resist, we have to assume that you are accepting a check from one of the corporations. There will probably be a Wikipedia page titled, "Plastic Politicians of the 21st Century". Here's your chance to keep off of that list.

Most forms of plastic production should be banned immediately, without any question or much debate. The more risk the plastic carries, the bigger the cost. There is absolutely no reason they do not pay to produce plastic, especially when they are making no effort to improve recyclability. They won't listen to the people, and they use the government as a shield. It's all being blamed on you, politicians.

There should only be a few types in production and like nuclear waste, every drop of the chemicals should be accounted for from beginning to end. Collect any plastic and allow the factories to reuse what is available. When the current supply expires, plastic will be a nightmarish memory waiting to be scooped from the ocean.

Here are the lies handed to the public by the worst perpetrators. Thank you, Reuters:

"Coca-Cola, Nestle and PepsiCo have struggled for decades to increase the share of recycled plastic in their packaging.

In 1990, PepsiCo introduced a new plastic bottle with 25% recycled content. By the end of that decade the company said its bottles no longer contained any recycled content.

Coca-Cola began making plastic bottles in the United States with 25% recycled plastic. It phased them out in 1994 due to high costs, officials said then.

Coke and Pepsi declined to comment on these past targets.

In 2008, Nestle, the company behind Nescafe coffee and Pure Life water, set a U.S.-wide goal to make water bottles out of 60% recycled plastic within a decade.

That's a goal the company says was never met. Nestle told Reuters it was an ambitious target that didn't get the groundswell of industry and policy-maker support it needed.

Coke and Nestle said it is hard to get the plastic they need from recycled sources; Nestle said it often pays a premium for recycled material.

All three companies made new pledges in 2018:

Coca-Cola set a target to hit 50% recycled content in all packaging by 2030. Currently, it's at 20%, and about half that rate for PET plastic, it told Reuters.

PepsiCo said it would use 25% recycled content in packaging by 2025. It told Reuters in September it had reached 4% as of 2019.

Nestle said it aims to use 15% recycled plastic in its packaging by 2025. The company told Reuters this is at 3% currently, up from 2% when it made the pledge."

If this is just too difficult to ban for another ten years, the producers of anything like plastic should be forced to provide legitimate recycling or incineration plants of their own and collect the material. Each piece of plastic should be treated like nuclear waste, because it is comparable. It is ludicrous for them to send toxic plastic out into society with no means of taking care of it.

It took ten years for DDT to effectively be banned, and looking back now, it seems like they must have been out of their minds to wait even one day. There are still useless Brownfield zones contaminated with DDT.

Coca-Cola, Pepsi, and Nestle have lied to the public for a very long. DowDupont and ExxonMobil have lied to us for even longer.

These companies are making politicians look stupid, don't you want to defend yourselves? They lied to you, made you look foolish, and now you have been made aware. It would be quite silly to let them keep the wool over your eyes. We can only ask so many times. We'll start as individuals; it's not asking a whole lot to meet us in the middle.

The only way things will change is if we hold everyone accountable as a society. If you see a buffet dumping out trays because the clock struck three, call them out. If you can see your neighbors have six trash bags and a tiny bin for recycle- say something. If there's a container made of something other than plastic, go for that one.

Let's repurpose the expression – see something, say something. Let's make it about the planet. We don't need to be violent, but if someone is being wasteful, they are destroying your home, making it worse for your children. This planet is home, and any other allegiance you feel to any part has no fight in this ring. We are human beings; we need to get over ourselves and realize the immense weight of our actions.

To be clear though, if nothing is done, the plastic battle will have to be violent. They are maliciously attacking the earth and we may be forced to be her soldiers. It's just the way it is. *Quick destruction of a few is more sensible than giving many the opportunity to ruin themselves.*

One more thing, I propose that the "Prove You Are Not A Robot" test is administered on national television to the executives at Covanta, Waste Management, Pacific Gas & Electric, Sysco, DowDupont, Pepsi, Coke, ExxonMobil, British Petroleum, Carnival Cruises, and Nestle. I guess there's no legal ground for that, but it would be fun.

I do not believe for one second that they were born of this Earth and are composed of the same organic matter we are. If they are, then we need a new name for this version of the human race. *Homo sapiens* vs. *homo economicus.* The war to end all wars.

The sci-fi movies usually test robots by showing them terrible things and checking if the subject feels compassion. Show them that video of that turtle with a straw in its nose. Show them the end of *Toy Story 3* when Andy gives all of his toys away.

This is the most real example of *You broke it, you bought it* that ever existed.

Nestle isn't going to put water inside of another plastic bottle. DowDupont, Pepsi, and Coca-Cola have agreed to halt production as well. The soda will still flow, don't worry. I was glad to hear this. It is sadistic; totally **fucked up** for a company which knowingly destroys the world to use a polar bear as its mascot.

The companies figuring out the proper way to sell it because they didn't even try before. The response has come before the legislation has even passed senate, and for that, let's give these companies a round of applause. Thank you for recognizing our cries and acknowledging them with intent. For the first time, I wouldn't mind pretending a corporation is a person.

To the corporations sharpening your public relation swords, take a step back and assess the situation. The people have been made aware of your crimes against us. You will stop using us for profit, you will cease destroying our planet. You have been warned but this doesn't need to be a fight. Research what happened to the DDT industry; most of you were part of it, so you already know. DowDupont, here you go again. I'm sure you'll find a new way to murder us all.

To the people, I will call upon an old movie. I'm not much of actor, but I can sure deliver this scene with passion that may win me an Academy Award. Its slogan should begin a conversation, in the very least.

I don't have to tell you things are bad. Everybody knows things are bad. It's a depression. Everybody's out of work, or scared of losing their job. The dollar buys a nickel's worth; banks are going bust, shopkeepers keep a gun under the counter, punks are running wild in the street, and there's nobody anywhere who seems to know what to do, and there's no end to it! We know the air is unfit to breathe and our food is unfit to eat, and we sit watching our TVs while some local newscaster tells us that today we had fifteen homicides and sixty-three violent crimes, as if that's the way it's supposed to be!

We know things are bad — worse than bad. They're crazy. It's like everything everywhere is going crazy, so we don't go out anymore. We sit in the house, and slowly the world we are living in is getting smaller, and all we say is: 'Please, at least leave us alone in our living rooms. Let me have my toaster and my TV and my steel-belted radials and I won't say anything. Just leave us alone.' Well, I'm not gonna leave you alone. I want you to get MAD! I don't want you to protest, I don't want you to riot, I don't want you to write to your congressman, because I wouldn't know what to tell you to write. I don't know what to do about the depression and the inflation and the Russians and the crime in the street. All I know is that first, you've got to get mad! You've got to say: 'I'm a human being, goddammit! My life has value!'

So, I want you to get up now. I want all of you to get up out of your chairs. I want you to get up right now and go to the window, open it, and stick your head out, and yell: I'M AS MAD AS HELL, AND I'M NOT GOING TO TAKE THIS ANYMORE! I want you to get up right now. Sit up. Go to your windows. Open them and stick your head out and yell: 'I'm as mad as hell and I'm not gonna take this anymore!' Things have got to change. But first, you've gotta get mad!...

You've got to say: I'M AS MAD AS HELL, AND I'M NOT GOING TO TAKE THIS ANYMORE! Then we'll figure out what to do about the depression and the inflation and the oil crisis! But first, get up out of your chairs, open the window, stick your head out, and yell, and say it: I'M AS MAD AS HELL, AND I'M NOT GOING TO TAKE THIS ANYMORE! Say it together, it is the new chant of a generation. I AM MAD AS HELL, AND I AM NOT GOING TO TAKE THIS ANYMORE.''

Thank you for the applause. In my dreams, all of you stood and chanted. I suppose I'm too idealist. The woman in the front row just took a sip from a plastic bottle.

In the words of John F. Kennedy, "Those who make peaceful revolution impossible will make violent revolution inevitable."

It's your call.

For the people, maybe the words of the lifted-Lorax are better, "Unless someone like you cares a whole awful lot, nothing is going to get better. It's not."

Now, will someone give me a ride home? Because there's most certainly an armed bomb waiting for me to turn the ignition.

They all laughed, but I'm calling a taxi. I really think I'm going to be murdered for this. I once read that laughter can kill anything, even murder. I always encourage a firm grip on the neck, but I am not into autoerotic-asphyxiation, don't let them try to tell you otherwise.

Fini.

<u>**Quotations:**</u>

The Truth
Incubus- *Warning - "Those left standing..."*

Native American Proverb - "*We do not inherit...*"
Daniel Quinn- *Ishmael* "*We're not destroying the world because...*"
Bob Dylan- *It's Alright Ma, I'm Only Bleeding* - "*If my thought-dreams...*"
The Beatles - *Your Mother Should Know*
Mary Poppins, 1964 - "*A teaspoon of sugar...*"

Maybe Baby (The Crickets)
Wall-E, 2008 "*There's plenty of space...*"
The X-Files, *"Aubrey"* - "*Dreams are questions...*"
Notting Hill, 1999 – "*I'm just a girl, standing in front of a boy, asking him to love her.*"
Full Metal Jacket, 1987 - "*I bet you're the kind of guy...*"
Funkadelic- *Maggot Brain* - "*Mother Earth is pregnant...*"

The Cook
Kurt Vonnegut- *Cat's Cradle*

The Journalist
William Randolph Hearst, maybe George Orwell. *"News is something..."*
Adorno, Horkheimer- *Dialect of Enlightenment: The Culture Industry "Those in charge no longer take much trouble..."*
Alan Moore- *Watchmen – "Who's watching..."*
Network, 1976 *"...newscaster telling us that today we had fifteen homicides..."*
Tom Petty- *The Last DJ –"All the boys upstairs wanna see..."*

Silent Spring
Bill Hornsby- *The Way It Is*
Ray Stevens- *Jeremiah Peabody's Polyunsaturated Quick-Dissolving Fast-Acting Pleasant-Tasting Green and Purple Pills*
Nestle- "*We're one of 70,000...*" *InTheseTimes.com*

What Happened?
Ten Years After- *I'd Love to Change The World*
The Beatles- *All You Need is Love*
Talking Heads- *Psycho Killer- "You're talking a lot..."*

The Seasons
Wookiefoot- *Junk Food* – *"I wonder if my carrots get jet-lag?*

The Volunteer
Neil Young- *Keep on Rockin' In The Free World*
Allman Brothers Band- *Melissa*
Waiting..., 2005 *"Push the fish, it's about to turn."*
The Main Ingredient- *Everybody Plays The Fool*
Edwin Starr- *War "War! What is it good for?"*

...the Fuck?
Ancient Egyptian proverb - *"One quarter of what you eat..."*

The Starving
Fleetwood Mac- *The Chain* – *"You would never..."; "Damn the dark..."*
Quotes from Presidents, 1963-2016, from PBS

The Speech
Kurt Vonnegut- *Cat's Cradle*
E.F. Schumacher- *Small is Beautiful* – *"Any intelligent fool..."*
Network, 1976 – *"I don't have to tell you things are bad..."*
Yevgeny Zamyatin- *We* – *"The quick destruction..."*
Dr. Seuss- *The Lorax* – *"Unless someone like you..."*

<u>**Organizations to thank for information:**</u>
Environmental Protection Agency
United States Department Of Agriculture
National Resources Defense Council
Feeding America
Recycle Track Systems
The Recycling Partnership
Bureau Of Labor & Statistics
National Waste & Recycling Association
World Wildlife Fund

Books:
Al Gore- *An Inconvenient Truth*
Edward Abbey- *The Monkey Wrench Gang*
Edward Humes- *Garbology*
Elizabeth Kolbert- *The Sixth Extinction*
Elizabeth Kolbert-*Field Notes From A Catastrophe*
Elizabeth Royte- *Garbage Land, or The Secret Trail of Trash*
Hunter Thompson - *Kingdom Of Fear*
John Stauber and Sheldon Rampton- *Toxic Sludge Is Good For You!*
John Stauber and Sheldon Rampton- *Trust Us, We're Experts*
Max Horkheimer and Theodor W. Adorno- *Dialectic of Enlightenment*
Michael Braungart and William McDonough- *Cradle to Cradle: Remaking the Way We Make Things*
Rachel Carson- *Silent Spring*
Stephen Fenichell- *Plastic: The Making of a Synthetic Century*
Susan Freinkel- *Plastic: A Toxic Love Story*
Susan Strasser- *Waste and Want: A Social History of Trash*
Upton Sinclair- *The Jungle*
Walter Benjamin- *The Work of Art in the Age of Mechanical Reproduction*
Walter Lippman and Gabriel Almond- *The Almond Lippman Consensus*

Media Outlets:
al-Jazeera
Associated Press
The Atlantic
Boston Globe
Canadian Broadcasting Channel
Columbia Journalism Review
Florida Sun-Sentinel
The Guardian
In These Times
National Geographic
NBC
New York Times
NPR
PBS
Reuters
Rolling Stone
Society of Professional Journalists
Time Magazine

Vice   Wikipedia
Washington Post

<u>Films and Television:</u>
An Inconvenient Truth   *Kooyanisqatsi*
An Inconvenient Sequel: Truth   *Oceans: The Mystery Of The*
to Power   *Missing Plastic*
At The Fork   *PLANEAT*
Blue Gold   *Plastic Wars*
Diet Fiction   *The Waking Life*
Food Choices   *Trashed! Jeremy Irons*
Food Fight   *Waiting…*
Forks Over Knives   *Wasted!*
Just Eat It!   *Waste Land*
Kitchen Nightmares

<u>BEWARE:</u>
*(Many of these organization's names are manipulative. For
    example- Californians for Recycling are actually plastic
    company representatives who lobby against recycling.)*
Californians for Recycling and the Environment
American Petroleum Institute
Americans For Prosperity
National Plastics Council
American Chemistry Council
Competitive Enterprise Institute
Waste Management
The American Forest & Paper Association
The Fnords

<u>List of principal sources:</u>

Al Jazeera. (2020, September 30). Toxins in plastic blamed for
    health, environment hazards. Retrieved October 06, 2020, from
    https://www.aljazeera.com/news/2020/9/30/toxins-in-plastics-
    blamed-for-health-environment-hazards

American Petroleum Institute. (2020, September 14). Retrieved
    October 06, 2020, from
    https://en.wikipedia.org/wiki/American_Petroleum_Institute

An Inconvenient Sequel: Truth To Power [Video file]. (2017).
    YouTube.

Benjamin, W., Zohn, H., & Arendt, H. (2019). *Illuminations: Essays
    and reflections*. Boston: Mariner Books, Houghton Mifflin
    Harcourt.

Blue Gold - World Water Wars. (n.d.). Retrieved October 06, 2020,
    from https://klamathlibrary.kanopy.com/video/blue-gold-
    world-water-wars-0

Braungart, M., & McDonough, W. (2019). *Cradle to cradle:
    Remaking the way we make things*. London: Vintage.

Carson, R. (1994). *Silent Spring*. Boston: Mifflin.

Covanta's Crimes. (n.d.). Retrieved October 06, 2020, from
    https://www.dioxinsontario.com/covanta-s-crimes

Cushman, J. (1994, October 06). CONGRESS FORGOES ITS BID
    TO HASTEN CLEANUP OF DUMPS. Retrieved October 06,
    2020, from https://www.nytimes.com/1994/10/06/us/congress-
    forgoes-its-bid-to-hasten-cleanup-of-dumps.html?scp=8

Dickinson, T. (2020, March 06). Planet Plastic. Retrieved October
    06, 2020, from https://www.rollingstone.com/culture/culture-
    features/plastic-problem-recycling-myth-big-oil-950957/

Diet Fiction: How the Diet Industry Makes People Fatter and Sicker
[Video file]. (2019). Amazon Prime.

Dunlap, D. (2012, November 03). Floodwater Pours Into 9/11
Museum, Hampering Further Work on the Site. Retrieved
October 06, 2020, from
https://www.nytimes.com/2012/11/03/nyregion/floodwater-
pours-into-9-11-museum-hampering-further-work-on-the-
site.html

Food Fight [Video file]. (2008). Amazon Prime.

Forks Over Knives [Video file]. (2011). Amazon Prime.

Freinkel, S. (2011). *Plastic: A Toxic Love Story*. Boston: Houghton
Mifflin Harcourt.

Fresh Kills Landfill. (2020, September 26). Retrieved October 06,
2020, from https://en.wikipedia.org/wiki/Fresh_Kills_Landfill

Freshkills Park. (2020, March 03). Retrieved October 06, 2020, from
https://en.wikipedia.org/wiki/Freshkills_Park

Frontline: Plastic Wars [Video file]. (2020). Amazon Prime.

Garbage Land: On the Secret Trail of Trash. (2010). Paw Prints.

Gore, A. (2007). *An Inconvenient Truth*. New York: Viking.

GP. (2011). Retrieved October 06, 2020, from
https://www.amazon.com/gp/video/detail/B081ZFB1VK/ref=a
tv_wl_hom_c_unkc_1_2

Green Career Articles. (2015, June 24). Retrieved October 06, 2020,
from https://www.bls.gov/green/greencareers.htm

Horkheimer, M., & Adorno, T. W. (1972). *Dialect Of
Enlightenment*. New York: Continuum.

How Large is the Carbon Footprint of Wasted Goods in the Food
Industry? – Logmore Blog. (n.d.). Retrieved October 06, 2020,
from https://www.logmore.com/post/food-industry-carbon-
footprint

Hyman, M. (2016). Eat fat, get thin: Why the fat we eat is the key to
sustained weight loss and vibrant health. Retrieved October 06,
2020, from https://www.amazon.com/Fat-Fiction-Dr-Mark-
Hyman/dp/B086844B7N/ref=pd_ys_iyr16

Just Eat It: A Food Waste Story [Video file]. (n.d.). Amazon Prime.
Retrieved 2014.

Kolbert, E. (2006). *Field notes from a catastrophe*. London:
Bloomsbury.

Lippard, L. (2016, October 28). New York comes clean: The
controversial story of the Fresh Kills dumpsite. Retrieved
October 06, 2020, from
https://www.theguardian.com/cities/2016/oct/28/new-york-
comes-clean-fresh-kills-staten-island-notorious-dumpsite

McCabe, K. (2008, April 20). Retrieved October 06, 2020, from
http://archive.boston.com/news/local/articles/2008/04/20/gettin
g_that_sinking_feeling/?page=full

National Waste & Recycling Association. (n.d.). Retrieved October
06, 2020, from
https://wasterecycling.org/news/523367/NWRA-JOINS-U.S.-
PLASTICS-PACT.htm

New horizons for sludge. (2020, January 20). Retrieved October 06,
2020, from
https://www.veoliawatertechnologies.com/en/newsroom/latest-
news/new-horizons-sludge

Oceans - The Mystery of the Missing Plastic. (n.d.). Retrieved
October 06, 2020, from
https://klamathlibrary.kanopy.com/video/oceans

Ortiz, E. (2020, October 04). 'We've been forgotten': In Newark, N.J., a toxic Superfund site faces growing climate threats. Retrieved October 06, 2020, from https://www.nbcnews.com/news/us-news/we-ve-been-forgotten-newark-n-j-toxic-superfund-site-n1240706

PLANEAT [Video file]. (2010). Amazon Prime.

Polypropylene Recycling Coalition. (n.d.). Retrieved October 06, 2020, from https://recyclingpartnership.org/polypropylene-coalition/

Quinn, D. (1995). *Ishmael*. New York: Bantam/Turner Book.

Rampton, S., & Stauber, J. (2002). *Trust us, we're experts!: How industry manipulates science and gambles with your future.* New York: Tarcher/Putnam.

Reports, S. (2020, October 05). The Plastic Pandemic: COVID-19 trashed the recycling dream. Retrieved October 06, 2020, from https://www.reuters.com/investigates/special-report/health-coronavirus-plastic-recycling/

Rubbermaid Food Storage Recycling Program. (n.d.). Retrieved October 06, 2020, from https://www.terracycle.com/en-US/brigades/rubbermaid-food-storage

Saving the Landfills. (1990, February 06). Retrieved October 06, 2020, from https://www.nytimes.com/1990/02/06/science/science-watch-saving-the-landfills.html?searchResultPosition=4

Semuels, A. (2020, February 26). The Plan to Make Producers Pay to Fix Recycling in the U.S. Retrieved October 06, 2020, from https://time.com/5790656/fixing-recycling-in-america/?utm_source=newsletter

Simpson, S. (2020, August 28). Why Is Monsanto Evil, but DuPont Isn't? Retrieved October 06, 2020, from https://www.investopedia.com/articles/investing/061913/why-monsanto-evil-dupont-isnt.asp

Sinclair, U. (1960). *Jungle*. New York: New American Library.

Small Towns vs. Nestlé. (n.d.). Retrieved October 06, 2020, from https://inthesetimes.com/article/small-towns-vs-nestle

Stauber, J. C., & Rampton, S. (2004). *Toxic sludge is good for you: Lies, damn lies and the public relations industry*. London: Constable & Robinson.

Strasser, S. (1999). *Waste And Want: A Social History Of Trash*. New York: Henry Holt.

Sullivan, L. (2020, September 11). How Big Oil Misled The Public Into Believing Plastic Would Be Recycled. Retrieved October 06, 2020, from https://www.npr.org/2020/09/11/897692090/how-big-oil-misled-the-public-into-believing-plastic-would-be-recycled

Sullivan, L. (2020, September 11). How Big Oil Misled The Public Into Believing Plastic Would Be Recycled. Retrieved October 06, 2020, from https://www.npr.org/2020/09/11/897692090/how-big-oil-misled-the-public-into-believing-plastic-would-be-recycled

Thompson, H. S. (2015). *Kingdom of fear: Loathsome secrets of a star-crossed child in the final days of the American century*. London: Penguin Books.

Tierney, J. (1996, June 30). Recycling Is Garbage. Retrieved October 06, 2020, from https://www.nytimes.com/1996/06/30/magazine/recycling-is-garbage.html

Toxic Sites. (n.d.). Retrieved October 06, 2020, from http://www.toxicsites.us/

Trashed with Jeremy Irons. (n.d.). Retrieved October 06, 2020, from
https://klamathlibrary.kanopy.com/video/trashed-0

United States 2030 Food Loss and Waste Reduction Goal. (2020,
September 15). Retrieved October 06, 2020, from
https://www.epa.gov/sustainable-management-food/united-
states-2030-food-loss-and-waste-reduction-goal

Veolia Water Technologies: About Us. (n.d.). Retrieved October 06,
2020, from
https://www.veoliawatertechnologies.com/en/about-us

Waste Land [Video file]. (2010). Sling.

Wasted! The Story of Food Waste [Video file]. (2017). Amazon
Prime.

Water & Wastewater Management Services - SUEZ in North
America. (2020, August 09). Retrieved October 06, 2020, from
https://www.suez-na.com/en-us

Weisskopf, M. (1986, November 16). Toxic-Waste Site Awash in
Misjudgment. Retrieved October 06, 2020, from
https://www.washingtonpost.com/archive/politics/1986/11/16/t
oxic-waste-site-awash-in-misudgment/4b46a5ae-2fcb-44d1-
a1bb-56bbf8a903da/

Woodward, A. (2020, October 04). Scientists engineered plastic-
eating 'super-enzymes' that can break down bottles in days.
Retrieved October 06, 2020, from
https://www.businessinsider.com/plastic-eating-super-enzyme-
recycles-plastic-bottles-2020-10

Screaming Spring Soundtrack

Incubus- *Warning*
Bob Dylan- *It's Alright Ma, I'm Only Bleeding*
The Beatles- *Your Mother Should Know*
The Stooges- *Greedy, Awful People*
Crosby, Stills & Nash- *Teach Your Children*
Antonio Vivaldi- "Spring" from *Four Seasons*
Ray Stevens- *Jeremiah Peabody's Polyunsaturated Quick-Dissolving Fast-Acting Pleasant-Tasting Green and Purple Pills*
Primus- *American Life*
Jimi Hendrix - *If 6 was 9*
The Mamas & The Papas- *California Dreamin'*
Ten Years After - *I'd Love to Change the World*
The Crickets- *Maybe Baby*
Neil Young- *Keep on Rockin' In The Free World*
Muse - *The 2nd Law: Unsustainable*
The Zombies- *Time of the Season*
Twiddle- *Polluted Beauty*
Public Enemy- *Fight the Power*

Bob Dylan- *Talking World War III Blues*
Louis Armstrong- *What a Wonderful World*
Talking Heads- *Cities*
Gil Scott-Heron- *The Revolution Will Not Be Televised*
Everlast- *What It's Like*
The Beatles- *All You Need Is Love*
Rage Against The Machine- *Wake Up*
Funkadelic- *Maggot Brain*
Ziggy Marley- *Dragonfly*
Reel Big Fish- *Sell Out*
Wookiefoot- *Junk Food*
Cornbugs- *Pigs are People, Too*
Supertramp- *The Logical Song*
Grateful Dead- *U.S. Blues*
Allman Brothers Band- *Whipping Post*
The Main Ingredient - *Everybody Plays The Fool*
Mike Love- *Permanent Holiday*

Richardsnickle25@gmail.com

www.ingramcontent.com/pod-product-compliance
Lightning Source LLC
Chambersburg PA
CBHW071212240726
48654CB00009B/751